SPURGEON ON THE POWER OF SCRIPTURE

SPURGEON ON THE POWER OF SCRIPTURE

Spurgeon Speaks, Vol. 2

Compiled by

Jason K. Allen

MOODY PUBLISHERS
CHICAGO

© 2021 by
Jason K. Allen

These sermons of Charles H. Spurgeon were originally published in the *Metropolitan Tabernacle Pulpit* and the *New Park Street Pulpit*. The compiler has sometimes shortened portions of these sermons and updated certain words and spelling for clarity and context. Scripture references have been updated to the New King James Version.

All Scripture quotations, unless otherwise indicated, are taken from the New King James Version. Copyright © 1982 by Thomas Nelson. Used by permission. All rights reserved.

Scripture quotations marked KJV are taken from the King James Version.

Emphasis in Scripture has been added.

Edited by Kevin Mungons
Interior Design: Brandi Davis
Cover Design: Gabriel Reyes-Ordeix
Cover illustration of Charles Spurgeon copyright © 2015 by denisk0/iStock (484302822). All rights reserved.

Library of Congress Cataloging-in-Publication Data

Names: Spurgeon, C. H. (Charles Haddon), 1834-1892, author. | Allen, Jason K., editor.
Title: Spurgeon on the power of scripture / [editor] Jason K. Allen.
Other titles: Sermons. Selections
Description: Chicago : Moody Publishers, [2021] | Series: Spurgeon speaks ; vol. 2 | Summary: "Volume 2 of the Spurgeon Speaks series focuses on the power of God's Word. Spurgeon's love for the Bible will encourage you too. Presented in lovely editions that you'll be proud to own, the series offers readings on topics of importance to the Prince of Preachers"-- Provided by publisher.
Identifiers: LCCN 2021009433 (print) | LCCN 2021009434 (ebook) | ISBN 9780802426291 | ISBN 9780802499585 (ebook)
Subjects: LCSH: Prayer--Christianity--Sermons.
Classification: LCC BV213 .S678 2021 (print) | LCC BV213 (ebook) | DDC 252--dc23
LC record available at https://lccn.loc.gov/2021009433
LC ebook record available at https://lccn.loc.gov/2021009434

Originally delivered by fleets of horse-drawn wagons, the affordable paperbacks from D. L. Moody's publishing house resourced the church and served everyday people. Now, after more than 125 years of publishing and ministry, Moody Publishers' mission remains the same—even if our delivery systems have changed a bit. For more information on other books (and resources) created from a biblical perspective, go to www.moodypublishers.com or write to:

Moody Publishers
820 N. LaSalle Boulevard
Chicago, IL 60610

3 5 7 9 10 8 6 4

Printed in the United States of America

Blessed is the man who has friends who are like brothers. Even more blessed is the man who has brothers who are also good friends. I am one such man, blessed with two older brothers who are also the closest of friends. I gratefully dedicate this book to one of those brothers, Marc Allen.

Contents

Introduction

BY JASON K. ALLEN

THOUGH BORN NEARLY 200 years ago, Charles Spurgeon remains, in the words of Carl F. H. Henry, "one of evangelical Christianity's immortals." Spurgeon's enduring stature is due to many reasons but, unquestionably, one of those is his pulpit ministry.

Spurgeon is often referred to as the Prince of Preachers. To put it in common parlance, Spurgeon was a preaching machine. He often preached up to ten times per week, each to packed church houses. Weekly, Spurgeon's sermons were quickly transcribed, edited, and then sent coursing throughout the world through the tentacles of the British Empire. Spurgeon's eloquence and evident spiritual power drew people, again and again, to hear him preach. Literally, multitudes flocked to him often overwhelming meeting houses and filling outdoor venues. Many found Spurgeon's preaching irresistible. In fact, in 1857, Spurgeon preached to a crowd numbering 23,654 at

London's Crystal Palace. By the end of his ministry, Spurgeon had preached to more than ten million people without the aid of modern technologies.

Spurgeon often cited prayer as the secret to his power in the pulpit. And indeed it was. But working in tandem with the prayers of God's people was Spurgeon's ironclad belief in the Bible as the inspired, infallible Word of God. Spurgeon preached the Scriptures with power because he believed the Scriptures were powerful. God blessed Spurgeon's preaching of the Word because Spurgeon believed the Bible was the Word of God. In Spurgeon's day, higher criticism was ravaging the church and undermining the confidence God's people placed in Scripture. Yet Spurgeon stood as a bulwark, prophetically pushing back against those who assailed Scripture.

And that's the point of this book, to give the reader a higher, more confident belief in Scripture. But my aim, as was Spurgeon's, is not to leave it in the abstract. Page by page, as your belief in Scripture is deepened, so will your faith, your perseverance, your confidence, and your joy. Your Christian life will be emboldened, as will your Christian service. Within this book you'll find seven of Spurgeon's sermons on the power of Scripture. They've been strategically selected and carefully edited, both for maximum impact on your Christian life.

The Word of God is both sweet as honey and sharp as a two-edged sword. It's our spiritual nourishment and our spiritual weapon. As you read this book and behold the multifaceted beauty of Scripture and apply it to your Christian life, your faith in Scripture—and in God Himself—will be strengthened, as will your life and ministry.

Spurgeon once quipped that he need not defend the Bible. He likened the Bible to a lion in a cage. It need not be defended, just let it out of the cage to defend itself. In these sermons, Spurgeon does just that—he unpacks the Scriptures in all their power. Using a similar analogy, Winston Churchill, reflecting afterward on his role in rallying the British people in the face of the Nazi threat, famously said, "It was the nation and the race, dwelling all around the globe, that had the lion's heart. I had the luck to be called on to give the roar."*

So it is with Spurgeon and Scripture. It is Holy Scripture that is powerful, but in these sermons, Spurgeon lets them out of their cage and gives them the roar. Read and be blessed.

---

* Winston Churchill, "Address to the House of Commons" (November 30, 1954), quoted in Bruce Bliven, *The World Changers* (New York: John Day Co., 1965), 125.

TITLE:

The Word of a King

TEXT:

Ecclesiastes 8:4

SUMMARY:

Because God is monarch, His Word has power. Spurgeon first shows how the power of the Word excites our awe of Him. He shows in creation and redemptive history the power of God spoken in His Word. Second, he highlights the power of the Word of God in ensuring our obedience to it. Third, the power of the Word inspires our confidence. If we struggle with remaining corruption, there is power in the Word of God to cleanse us. Fourth, the power of the Word directs our efforts. We need the Word of God to do the work of God.

NOTABLE QUOTES

"Christians should more diligently search the Word to find out what the will of the Lord is on all matters affecting their everyday life."

"We should tremble at God's Word, and humble ourselves in the dust before Him, praying to be cleansed by His grace."

"Spiritual work can only be done by spiritual power."

A sermon preached by Charles H. Spurgeon on March 22, 1873. *Metropolitan Tabernacle Pulpit*, vol. 19.

1

The Word of a King

Where the word of a king is, there is power.

ECCLESIASTES 8:4

KINGS IN SOLOMON'S DAY had a vast amount of power, for their word was absolute. They did according to their own will, and none could check them, for, as Solomon said, "The wrath of a king is like the roaring of a lion; Whoever provokes him to anger sins against his own life" (Prov. 20:2). When such a monarch happened to be wise and good, it was a great blessing to the people; for "a king who sits on the throne of judgment scatters all evil with his eyes" (Prov. 20:8). But if he was of a hard, tyrannical nature, his subjects were mere slaves and groaned beneath a yoke of iron.

We do not sufficiently give thanks for the blessings of a constitutional government, but if we were for a season put beneath the power of a grinding despotism, we should set more store by those liberties for which we have to thank our Puritan ancestors. Mercies are seldom appreciated till they are taken away.

May we not prove ungrateful under free institutions, for if so, we shall be more brutish than any men.

There is, however, one King whose power we do not wish in any degree to limit or circumscribe. God does as He wills among the armies of heaven and the inhabitants of this lower world. None can stay His hand or say to Him, "What are you doing?" In this we greatly rejoice. The personal rule of one individual would be the best form of government if that individual were perfectly good, infinitely wise, and abundant in power. An autocrat turns into a despot because there is no man who is perfectly good, unselfish, or wise.

God has no fault or failing, and therefore it is a joy that He does according to His will. He never wills anything that is not strictly just; He is neither unjust nor unmerciful. He cannot err, and therefore it is a great subject for joy that "the LORD reigns" (Ps. 93:1).

Now, because God is the absolute Monarch, His word has power about it, and of that word of power I am going to speak at this time. May the Holy Spirit help us to think of the power of God's word for four purposes—first, to excite our awe; second, to ensure our obedience; third, to inspire our confidence; and fourth, to direct our efforts.

EXCITE OUR AWE

First, we would see the power of the Word of the Lord in order to excite our awe of Him. What are we poor creatures of a day? What is there in us as we appear in God's sight? Do we not pass away as the flower of the field? As for our word, what is it? We sometimes talk exceedingly proudly, and we say "shall" and "will" as if we could do anything when, after all, our word is but breath, a vapor, a mere sound in the air. Man proposes, but God disposes; man resolves, but God dissolves. That which man expects, God rejects, for the Word of the Lord stands forever, but man passes away and is not.

Think of the day before all days when there was no day but the Ancient of Days, and when God dwelled all alone, then He willed in His mind that there should be a world created: "By the word of the LORD the heavens were made, And all the host of them by the breath of His mouth" (Ps. 33:6). What a word is that which created all things! And remember that this same word can destroy all things, for "the heavens and the earth which are now preserved by the same word, are reserved for fire until the day of judgment and perdition of ungodly men" (2 Peter 3:7). If He were but to speak, all things that are would melt away as a moment's foam dissolves into the wave that bears it and is lost forever.

When the Lord created, He used no hand of cherubim or seraphim. All that we read in the sublimely simple record of Genesis is, "God said, let there be," and there was. His word accomplished all, and when He wills to destroy either one man or a million, His word is able to work His will. What a mighty word cut off the host of Sennacherib and slew the firstborn of Egypt! The word of the Lord commanded the floodwaters, and they drowned a guilty world, and that same word rained fire from heaven upon Sodom and Gomorrah. Even so in the last day; when the word shall go forth from Him, He shall shake not only the earth but also heaven, and at His word of power both heaven and earth shall flee away. Great God, we do adore you, for you are both Creator and Destroyer by your word!

Think how God's word both makes alive and kills. He promised Abraham that he should have a seed in whom all the nations of the earth should be blessed. It seemed impossible that there should come from him a son that should be the founder of a race—his body was dead, and Sarah was old—yet God in due time made them to laugh, for Isaac was born into the house.

It is the Lord who makes alive, and equally it is the Lord who kills. It only needs God to will it, and the pestilence lays men low in heaps like the grass of the meadow when the mower's scythe has passed over it. The Lord has but to call for pestilence or war, and myriads of men are laid low. If He wills to chasten by famine, He calls for devouring insects, and they invade the land. Oh, how we ought to worship you, you dread Supreme, upon whose word life and death are made to hang!

I might in another division of this part of my subject remind you of the power which attends both His promises and His threatenings. God has never promised without performing in due time to the last jot and tittle. Has He said, and shall He not do it? Has He commanded, and shall it not come to pass? The gifts and calling of God are without repentance; He turns not from His covenant engagements and swerves not from the performance of His word.

Those who have resisted Him have found His threatenings to be true also: let Pharaoh confess how the plagues followed fast upon the word of the Lord till even his stout heart was melted within him. Men have gone on for a while resisting God and in their pride have laughed Him to scorn, but by-and-by He has spoken to them in His wrath and vexed them in His hot displeasure. Who can stand against this terrible God, whose word overthrows the mighty and casts the proud beneath His feet?

There is power in God's word to foretell so that, when He tells what is to be in the future, we know that it shall come to pass. Thus says the Lord, "Indeed I have spoken it; I will also bring it to pass. I have purposed it; I will also do it" (Isa. 46:11). In the word of the Lord also there is power to predestinate as well as to foretell so that what He decrees is fixed and certain. The Lord has said it, "My counsel shall stand, and I will do all My pleasure" (Isa. 46:10). Let this be your joy today, that whatever is promised of the latter day and of the glory that is to be revealed, is sure to come to pass, for the mouth of the Lord has spoken it.

It seems impossible that the heathen should ever be the Lord's or that the uttermost parts of the earth should be Christ's possession, but it will be, for the King has said it, and "Where the word of a king is, there is power." We fear that the time will never arrive when peace shall reign through all the world, and when men shall hang the helmet in the hall and study war no more; but the vision of faith shall yet become a fact, for, "Where the word of a king is, there is power."

He spoke of old of Edom and Moab, Philistia and Ammon, Nineveh and Babylon, Greece and Borne, and whatsoever He has spoken has been fulfilled. Not one word of the prophecies of Daniel and Ezekiel has failed of its accomplishment, and we may be sure that not one glorious vision of the seer of Patmos will remain a dream. Let us worship the great Ordainer, Benefactor, and Ruler, whose every word is the word of a King, in which there is power.

ENSURE OUR OBEDIENCE

Second, we would think of the power of God's word in order to ensure our obedience to it. Whenever God gives a word of command, it comes to us clothed with authority, and its power over our minds should be immediate and unquestioned. I hope that in laying the foundation of the spiritual building that is to be erected in connection with this place you will take care to do it according to the directions of the divine statute book. One is our Master, even Christ, and we must do our Master's will, not our own.

Some Christian people do not view the authority of God's word as paramount but instead consult human leaders or their predilections. This is to begin with the word of man, a weak and sandy foundation; I beseech you—do not so. To Christians the word of God is the only rule of faith and practice. Our doctrine is of authority because it is God's word, and for no other reason. Our ordinances are valid because instituted by God's word; they are idle ceremonies if they be not so commanded. All the rites, rules, and regulations of man are of no value.

The book of human decrees is not to be regarded in the church of Christ. You may put in the front of it, "printed by authority," but to the church of Christ it has no authority. You may adopt a creed as the standard of any particular church, but that gives it no authority to bind the conscience. It may be authorized by princes, bishops, and holy men, but wherein it differs from the Word of the Lord, or adds thereto, it is to the children of God as a puff of wind. The sole authority in the church is Christ Himself; He is the head of His church, and His word is the only authority by which we are ruled, for "where the word of a king is, there is power." But all are usurpers who act as lords in the church where Jesus alone is Master and Lord.

Christians should more diligently search the word to find out what the will of the Lord is on all matters affecting their everyday life. A loyal subject of the great King wants to know what the King would have him do; when he knows it, it is not for him to question or to cavil but to obey. Brethren, let us obey in all things the King's Word, and give to His holy Word the honor that it justly claims, for "where the word of a king is, there is power." Every precept that He gives He intends us to keep. He does not ordain it that we may question it; He commands that we may obey.

Let me refer you to what Solomon says in Ecclesiastes 8:2, "I say, 'Keep the king's commandment.'" This is admirable counsel for every Christian; if the commandment were of men, even the wisest of men, we might break it, and perhaps do right in breaking it. But if it be the King who gives the command, even the Lord Jesus Christ, who is the King in Zion, then the advice of the Preacher is wise and weighty.

Perhaps some of you would ask me, "What is the best course for me to pursue in certain difficult cases?" "Keep the King's commandment." If He be a King, then it is a solemn hazard to your soul if you come short of the least of His commandments. Remember that one treason makes a traitor; one leak sinks a ship; one fly spoils the whole box of ointment. He that bought us with His blood deserves to be obeyed in all things with all our heart, mind, soul, and strength. Such a King as we have ought never to hear us ask the reason why He commands.

Solomon goes on to say, "Do not be hasty to go from his presence" (Eccl. 8:3). There is such power in God's word that I would have you also obey this precept and seek to remain in His presence. Some of His people seek to get away from their Lord instead of keeping close to Him. So little do they delight in communion with their God that they seem to say, "Where can I go from Your Spirit? Or where can I flee from Your presence?" (Ps. 139:7).

Did it never happen to you as it did to Jonah, when he must needs go to Tarshish, though the Lord told him to go to Nineveh? He did not want such a large field of labor, such an anxious and unremunerative post of duty. He would rather go to a village or a seaside place. For a time he believed that providence helped him, for he found a ship going to Tarshish. There are many devil's providences that make sin easy and obedience difficult. The precept, not the providence, is the rule of duty. The providence that gave Judas the opportunity to sell his Master did not excuse that son of perdition. Alas, poor Jonah, to be thus eager to run counter to the word of a King!

I remember how I felt when first in London: I could not endure the horrible wilderness of bricks by which I was surrounded. I sighed for the green fields and the fresh air and longed to get back to my country charge. But this kind of self-indulgence will not do: "Where the word of a king is, there is power," and wherever the King sends you, you must go, and go without questioning. If He should send you to preach at the gates of hell, go and preach there.

"Do not be hasty to go from his presence," for if you get out of the sight of the King, if you no longer wait in His blessed presence, depend upon it, like Jonah you will fall into trial, tempest, sinking, and terror. There may be no whale to swallow you and cast you up again—they are not so plentiful now as they were then—and you may not be delivered so easily as Jonah. Keep in the Lord's presence and favor, no matter where you may have to go in order to do so. Walk in communion with Christ in whatever path He may point out to you. Never mind how rough it is. Do not imagine it is the wrong road because it is so rough; rather, reckon it to be right because it is rough, for seldom do smoothness and rightness go together. Oh, to abide in Christ the Word and to have His word abiding in us!

Solomon then says, "Do not take your stand for an evil thing." There is such power in the Word of God that He can readily destroy you or heavily chastise you, therefore be quick to amend, and "do not take your stand for an evil thing." Repent, obey, submit, confess, seek pardon at once. If at any time you offend against your gracious Sovereign, and He frown on you, humble yourself, for His stroke is heavy.

Have a tender mouth; let God guide you with His eye, let a word be enough for you, do not need a bit or bridle. I wish we all had great tenderness of conscience. We should tremble at God's Word and humble ourselves in the dust before Him, praying to be cleansed by His grace. Sin should be impossible to a believer who lives in the presence of the King, in whose word there is power. Will you offend Him to His face and slight Him in His own courts? No; yield yourself to His mercy and let your holy life prove that His word has power over your heart and conscience.

INSPIRE OUR CONFIDENCE

And now, third, to inspire our confidence, let us think that "where the word of a king is, there is power." The word of His is not a mere sound; there is the power of truth in it. If you do what He bids, you shall find that He can and will abundantly pardon. Whatever sins you have committed, though they are too many to count and too awful to mention, if you will come and trust yourself with Jesus Christ, God's word is that you shall be saved; and saved you shall be. "He who believes in the Son has everlasting life" (John 3:36). Come and plead these words now, you who feel your sinfulness, and you shall prove in your joyful experience that they are the power of God unto salvation. Even the very worst may come and plead the promises, and they shall obtain immediate pardon and full forgiveness, and their soul shall know it because of the sweet peace that comes from forgiven sin.

Do you tell me that you cannot conquer your evil passions and corrupt desires? Here is a promise from the Word of the Lord: "I will cleanse you from all your filthiness and from all your idols. I will give you a new heart and put a new spirit within you" (Ezek. 36:25–26). Come and plead these precious promises; there is power in them. They are the words of a King, and if you plead them at the mercy seat, you shall become a new creature in Christ Jesus. Old things shall pass away; all things shall become new.

When you get a promise from God, treat it as undoubted truth and rely upon it as you do upon the promise of your father or friend. Though there are men around you whose promises you never can believe, God's word is not like that of false and fickle mortals. No charge of falsehood or failure can be brought against the God of truth. He has never broken His word yet, and He never will. Then, dear souls, if you want forgiveness of sin and renewal of heart, get the promise to that effect and believe it with all your soul. As sure as it is the word of a King you shall be washed in the blood and in the water that flowed from the wounded side of the crucified Christ.

And you, Christian people, are you struggling at this time with a remaining corruption you cannot conquer? Come, lay hold of the promise that you shall overcome, and plead it before the mercy seat. If you do but get any promise of God suited to your case, make quick use of it for there is power in it; it is the word of a King! The promise of the Lord will bear the weight of sin and justice, life and death, judgment and hell. Lean your whole weight on the word, and you shall find it to be like Mount Zion which cannot be removed but abides forever.

For my own part, I have no shadow of a hope but in the Word of the Lord; His Spirit has delivered me from all reliance upon duties, or feelings, or experiences. The Word of the Lord is the life of my soul. In the words of King Jesus, there is power to save you, to renew you, to pardon you, to preserve you, to sanctify you, and to perfect you. If you have hold on the promises, they will hold you for time and eternity too.

Then, also, are there any of you in great trouble? I cannot know all your cases, but if any one of you has a trial that you could not tell or a trouble that nobody could help you out of, go and spread it before the Lord. Remember His Word, "Many are the afflictions of the righteous, but the LORD delivers him out of them all" (Ps. 34:19). Go and tell Him that He has thus spoken and that He has therein pledged Himself to deliver you out of all afflictions. Be sure of this, He will be as good as His Word.

Do you expect soon to die? Are you somewhat distressed because sickness is undermining your constitution? Be not afraid, for His Spirit teaches you to sing, "Yea, though I walk through the valley of the shadow of death, I will fear no evil; for You are with me; Your rod and Your staff, they comfort me" (Ps. 23:4). Go and tell the Lord of His own Word, and you will look forward to death without fear.

Brethren, one more point is gained concerning the fear of death when we remember that the voice of a King will recall our bodies from the grave, and, "where the word of a king is, there is power." Do we ask mournfully as we survey the grave-yard, "Can these dry bones live?" We are not slow to answer with assurance of faith. He who brought again from the dead our Lord Jesus, that great Shepherd of the sheep, will also bring forth from their sepulchers all His sheep: "If the Spirit of Him who raised Jesus from the dead dwells in you, He who raised

Christ from the dead will also give life to your mortal bodies through His Spirit who dwells in you" (Rom. 8:11). We do not doubt this when we remember that with the trump of the archangel shall also be heard the voice of God, which voice shall speak the word omnipotent.

DIRECT YOUR EFFORTS

Fourth, my text is to be used to direct your efforts. You need power; not the power of money, or mind, or influence, or numbers; but "power from on high" (Luke 24:49). All other power may be desirable, but this power is indispensable. Spiritual work can only be done by spiritual power. I counsel you in order to get spiritual power in all that you do to keep the King's commandment, for "where the word of a king is, there is power." Lay not a stone of your spiritual church without His overseeing; do all things according as He has ordained. Regard Him as the wise Master-builder, and be all of you under the command of His word.

The day comes when much that has been built shall be destroyed, for the fire will try every man's work of what sort it is. It is easy to heap up a church with wood, hay, and stubble, which the fire will soon destroy; and it is very hard work to build one up with gold, silver, and precious stones, for these are rare materials and must be diligently sought for, laboriously prepared, and carefully guarded. The materials that will stand the fire of temptation, trial, death, and the like are not to be brought together by any word but the Word of the Lord.

But these alone are worth having. I would sooner have half a dozen Christian people truly spiritual and obedient to the Word of the Lord in all things than I would have half a dozen thousands of nominal Christians who neither care about the Word nor the King.

If you want power, keep the King's commandment, keep close to it in all things, and make it the law of your house and the motto of your flag. Wherein you go beyond the word, you go beyond the power, and wherein you stop short of the word, you also stop short of the power. In the King's word there is power, and you will have power as long as you keep to it. Real power is nowhere else to be found. Let us take care that we do not look elsewhere for power, for that will be leaving the fountains of living waters to hew out to ourselves broken cisterns that hold no water.

I fear that some Christian people have been looking in many other directions for the power that can only be found in the word of the King. At one time we were told that power lay in an educated ministry. This superstition has suffered many a blow from the manifest successes of those whose only language is the grand old Saxon. Then the cry was, "Well, really, we do not want these men of education; we need fluent speakers, men who can tell a great many anecdotes and stories. These are men of power." I hope we shall outgrow this delusion also. The Lord works by either of these classes of men, or by others who have not the qualifications of either of them, or by another sort of men, or fifty sorts of men, so long as they keep to the word of the King, in which there is power.

There is power in the gospel if it be preached by a man utterly without education: unlearned men have done great things by the power of the word. The polished doctor of divinity has been equally useful when he has kept to his Master's word. But if either of these has forgotten to make Christ's word first and last, the preaching has been alike powerless, whether uttered by the illiterate or the profound.

Others have thought it necessary, in order to have power among the masses, that there should be fine music. An organ is nowadays thought to be the power of God, and a choir is a fine substitute for the Holy Ghost. They have tried that kind of thing in America, where solos and quartets enable singing men and singing women to divide their services between the church and the theatre. Some churches have paid more attention to the choir than to the preaching. I do not believe in it. If God had meant people to be converted in that way, He would have sent them a command to attend the music halls and operas, for there they will get far better music than we can hope to give them. If there be charms in music to change the souls of men from sin to holiness, and if the preaching of the gospel will not do it, let us have done with Peter and Paul, with Chalmers and with Chrysostom, and let us exalt Mozart and Handel into their places, and let the great singers of the day take the places of the pleaders for the Lord. Even this would not content the maniacs of this age, for with the music room they crave the frippery of the theatre.

Combine with philosophy the sweet flowers of oratory, and then you can exclaim, with the idolaters of old, "These be thy gods, O Israel" (Exod. 32:4 KJV). Men are now looking for omnipotence in toys. But we do not believe it. We come back to this, "Where the word of a king is, there is power," and while we are prepared to admit that all and everything that has to do with us can be the vehicle of spiritual power if God so wills, we are more than ever convinced that God has spiritual power to give by His word alone. We must keep to the King's word if we desire to have this spiritual power for the Lord's work.

Whatsoever you find in Scripture to be the command of the King, follow it, though it leads you into a course that is hard for the flesh to bear: I mean a path of singular spirituality, and nonconformity to the world. Remember that, after all, the truth may be with the half dozen and not with the million. Christ's power may be with the handful as it was at Pentecost, when the power came down upon the despised disciples, and not upon the chief priests and scribes, though they had the sway in religious matters.

If we want to win souls for Christ, we must use the Word of God to do it. Other forms of good work languish unless the gospel is joined with them. Set about reforming, civilizing, and elevating the people, and you will lose your time unless you evangelize them. The total abstinence movement is good, and I would that all would aid it, but it affects little unless the gospel furnishes the motive and the force. The rod works no wonder till Moses grasps it, and moral teaching has small force till Jesus operates by it.

Those who doubt the power of the gospel and leave it for other forms of hopeful good leave strength for weakness, omnipotence for insufficiency. More and more I am persuaded that it is where the word of a King is that there is power, and all the rest is feebleness until that word has infused might into it. Everyone must buy his own experience, but mine goes to prove to me that the direct and downright preaching of the gospel is the most profitable work that I ever engage in: it brings more glory to God and good to men than all lecturing and addressing upon moral subjects. I should always, if I were a farmer, like to sow that seed that would bring me in the best return for my labor. Preaching the gospel is the most paying thing in the world; it is remunerative in the very highest sense. May your minister stick to the gospel, the old-fashioned gospel, and preach nothing else but Jesus Christ and Him crucified. If people will not hear that, do not let them hear anything at all; it is better to be silent than to preach anything else. Paul said, and I will say the same, "I determined not to know anything among you except Jesus Christ and Him crucified" (1 Cor. 2:2).

Then again, if you want power, you must use this Word in pleading. If your work here is to be a success, there must be much praying; everything in God's house is to be done with prayer. Give me a praying people, and I shall have a powerful people. The Word of the Lord gives power to our prayers. There is power in accepting that word, in getting it into you or receiving it. You never keep the truth till you have received this word of a King into your spiritual being and absorbed it into your spiritual nature. Oh, that you might every one of you eat the Word, live on it, and make it your daily food!

And then, there is power in the practicing of it. Where there is life through the King's word, it will be a strong life. The sinner's life is a feeble life; but an obedient life, an earnest Christian life, is a life of strength. Even those who hate it and abhor it cannot help feeling that there is a strange influence about it which they cannot explain, and they must respect it.

You will see its power in this place; I know you will see it, for you are resolved in God's strength that it shall be so. You will see its power to fill the place. There is nothing so attractive as the gospel of Christ. That one silver bell of the gospel has more melody in it than can be drawn from all the bells in all the steeples in the world. There is more sweetness in that one name Jesus than in all the harps of angels, let alone the music of men. When Jesus Christ's deity is denied in any chapel, it soon becomes a howling wilderness. If Christ, the Son of God, is gone, all is gone.

When you preach the gospel, souls will be saved. To secure that end, you must stick to the gospel, for that is the one means ordained by God for the conversion of sinners. We must teach the King's word if our work is to be blessed to the salvation of souls. We must plough with the law, and let the people know what sin means and what repentance means. Then we may hopefully sow them with the gospel. Some time ago we were told that there was no need of repentance, and that repentance only meant a change of mind, but what a tremendous change of mind true repentance does mean! Never speak lightly of repentance.

Then, too, the preaching of the truth, and the whole truth, will bring a power of union among you so that you who love the Lord will be heartily united. When Christian people quarrel, it is generally because they do not get sufficient spiritual food.

Dogs fight when there are no bones, and church members fall out when there is no spiritual food. We must give them plenty of gospel, for the gospel has the power of sweetening the temper and making us put up with one another.

Preach the King's word, for it will give you power in private prayer, power in the Sunday school, power in the prayer meeting, power in everything that you do because you will live upon the King's own word, and His Word is meat to the soul.

TITLE:

The Bible Tried and Proved

TEXT:

Psalm 12:6

SUMMARY:

It is marvelous that God has condescended to give us His written Word. Spurgeon first considers *the quality of the Word of God*. It is uniform in character with no contradictions. Second, Spurgeon considers the *trials of the Word of God*. It has been tested in every way and still stands. Third, Spurgeon examines the *claims of the Word of God*. They are to be studied, obeyed, and observed.

NOTABLE QUOTES

"In the whole Book, from Genesis to Revelation, the words of the Lord are found, and they are always pure words."

"These words of God are a firm foundation, and our eternal hopes are wisely built thereon."

A sermon preached by Charles H. Spurgeon on May 5, 1889. *Metropolitan Tabernacle Pulpit*, vol. 35.

2

The Bible Tried and Proved

The words of the LORD are pure words, like silver tried in a furnace of earth, purified seven times.

PSALM 12:6

IN THIS PSALM, OUR TEXT stands in contrast with the evil of the age. The psalmist complains that the "godly man ceases! For the faithful disappear from among the sons of men" (Ps. 12:1). It was a great grief to him, and he found no consolation except in the words of the Lord. What if men fail? The Word of the Lord abides! What a comfort it is to quit the arena of controversy for the green pastures of revelation! One feels like Noah when, shut within the ark, he saw no longer the death and desolation that reigned outside. Live in communion with the Word of God, and in the absence of Christian friends, you will not lack for company.

Furthermore, the verse stands in fuller contrast still with the words of the ungodly when they rebel against God and oppress

His people. They said, "With our tongue we will prevail; our lips are our own: who is lord over us?" (Ps. 12:4). They boasted, they domineered, they threatened. The psalmist turned away from the voice of the boaster to the words of the Lord. He saw the promise, the precept, and the doctrine of pure truth, and these consoled him. He had not so many of the words of the Lord as we have, but what he had he made his own. In the good company of those who had spoken under divine direction, he was able to bear the threats of those who surrounded him.

So, dear friend, if at any time your lot is cast where the truths you love so well are despised, get back to the prophets and apostles, and hear through them what God will speak. The voices of earth are full of falsehood, but the word from heaven is pure. There is a good practical lesson in the position of the text; learn it well. Make the Word of God your daily companion, and then, whatever may grieve you in the false doctrine of the hour, you will not be too much cast down, for the words of the Lord will sustain your spirit.

Looking at the text, does it not strike you as a marvel of condescension that the Lord, the infinite, should use words? He has arranged for us, in His wisdom, this way of communicating with one another. But as for Himself, He is pure spirit and boundless. Shall He contract His glorious thoughts into the narrow channel of sound, and ear, and nerve? Must the eternal mind use human words? The glorious Lord spoke worlds. The heavens and the earth were the utterances of His lips. To Him it seems more in accordance with His nature to speak tempests and thunders than to stoop to the humble vowels and consonants of a creature of the dust.

Will He in very deed communicate with man in man's own way? Yes, He stoops to speak to us by words. We bless the Lord for verbal inspiration, of which we can say, "I have treasured the words of His mouth more than my necessary food" (Job 23:12). I do not know of any other inspiration, neither am I able to conceive of any which can be of true service to us. We need a plain revelation upon which we can exercise faith.

If the Lord had spoken to us by a method in which His meaning was infallible but His words were questionable, we should have been puzzled rather than edified, for it is a task indeed to separate the true sense from the doubtful words. We would always be afraid that the prophet or apostle had not, after all, given us the divine sense. It is easy to hear and to repeat words, but it is not easy to convey the meaning of another into perfectly independent words of your own; the meaning easily evaporates. But we believe that holy men of old, though using their own language, were led by the Spirit of God to use words which were also the words of God. The divine Spirit so operated upon the spirit of the inspired writer that he wrote the words of the Lord, and we, therefore, treasure up every one of them.

Our condescending God is so well pleased to speak to us by words that He has even deigned to call His only begotten Son "the Word" (John 1:14). The Lord uses words not with reluctance but with pleasure, and He would have us think highly of them, too.

We believe we have the words of God preserved for us in the Scriptures. We are exceedingly grateful that it is so. If we had not the words of the Lord thus recorded, we should have felt that we lived in an evil time, since neither voice nor oracle is heard today. I say, we should have fallen upon evil days if the words that God spoke of old had not been recorded under His superintendence.

With this book before us, what the Lord spoke two thousand years ago He speaks now. His Word abides forever, for it was spoken for all ages. The Word of the Lord is so instinct with everlasting life and eternal freshness that it is as vocal and forceful in the heart of the saint today as it was to the ear of Abraham when he heard it in Canaan; or to the mind of Moses in the desert; or to David when he sang it to his harp.

I thank God that many of us know what it is to hear the divine Word re-spoken in our souls! By the Holy Ghost, the words of Scripture come to us with a present inspiration: not only has the Book been inspired, it is inspired. This Book is more than paper and ink; it talks with us. Was not that the promise, "When thou awakest, it shall talk with thee" (Prov. 6:22 kjv)? We open the Book with this prayer, "Speak, Lord, for Your servant hears" (1 Sam. 3:9), and we often close it with this feeling: "Here I am, for you called me" (1 Sam. 3:6). As surely as if the promise had never been uttered before, but the Lord has made Holy Scripture to be His direct word to our heart and conscience. May the Holy Spirit at this hour speak to you yet again!

THE QUALITY OF THE WORDS OF GOD

"The words of the Lord are pure words." From this statement, I gather, first, the uniformity of their character. No exception is made to any of the words of God, but they are all described as "pure words." They are not all of the same character—some are for teaching, others are for comfort, and others for rebuke—but they are all "pure words."

I conceive it to be an evil habit to make preferences in Holy Scripture. We must preserve this volume as a whole. Those sin against Scripture who delight in doctrinal texts but omit the consideration of practical passages. But remember that men of God in old time took great delight in the commands of the Lord. They respected the Lord's precepts, and they loved His law. If any refuse to hear of duties and ordinances, I fear that they do not love God's Word at all. He who does not love it all loves it not at all. On the other hand, they are equally mistaken who delight in the preaching of duties but care not for the doctrines of grace. They say, "That sermon was worth hearing, for it has to do with daily life." I am very glad that they are of this mind, but if they refuse other teaching of the Lord, they are greatly faulty. I fear you are not of God if you account a portion of the Lord's words to be unworthy of your consideration. Beloved, we prize the whole range of the words of the Lord. We do not set aside the histories any more than the promises.

Above all, do not drop into the semi-blasphemy of some, who think the New Testament vastly superior to the Old. I would not err by saying that in the Old Testament you have more of the bullion of truth than in the New, for therein I should be falling into the evil that I condemn. But this I will say: they are of equal authority, and they cast such light upon each other that we could not spare either of them. "Therefore what God has joined together, let not man separate" (Mark 10:9). In the whole Book, from Genesis to Revelation, the words of the Lord are found, and they are always pure words.

Neither is it right for any to say, "Thus spoke Christ himself; but such-and-such a teaching is Pauline." Nay, it is not Pauline; if it be here recorded, it is of the Holy Ghost. Whether the Holy Ghost speaks by Isaiah, or Jeremiah, or John, or James, or Paul, the authority is still the same. Even concerning Jesus Christ our Lord this is true; for He says of Himself, "The word which you hear is not Mine but the Father's who sent Me" (John 14:24). In this matter, He puts Himself upon the level of others who were as the mouth of God.

We accept the words of the apostles as the words of the Lord, remembering what John said: "We are of God. He who knows God hears us; he who is not of God does not hear us. By this we know the spirit of truth and the spirit of error" (1 John 4:6). A solemn judgment is thus pronounced upon those who would set the Spirit of Jesus against the Spirit that dwelled in the apostles. The words of the Lord are not affected in their value by the medium through which they came. Revealed truth is all of the same quality even when the portions of it are not of the same weight of metal.

We observe, next, the purity of the words of the Lord: "The words of the LORD are pure words." In commerce there is silver, and silver, as you all know: silver with alloy, and silver free from baser metal. The Word of God is the silver without the dross; it is as silver that has been purified seven times in a crucible of earth in the furnace till every worthless particle has been removed. It is absolutely pure.

It is truth in the form of goodness without admixture of evil. The commandments of the Lord are just and right. Perversions are possible and probable, but the Book itself is preeminently pure. Details are given of gross acts of criminality, but they leave no injurious impress upon the mind. The saddest story of Holy Scripture is a beacon and never a lure. This is the cleanest, clearest, purest Book extant among men; nay, it is not to be mentioned in the same hour with the fabulous records that pass for holy books. It comes from God, and every word is pure.

It is also a book pure in the sense of truth, being without admixture of error. I do not hesitate to say that I believe that there is no mistake whatever in the original Holy Scriptures from beginning to end. There may be, and there are, mistakes of translation, for translators are not inspired. Even the historical facts are correct. Doubt has been cast upon them here and there, and at times with great show of reason—doubt that has been impossible to meet for a season, but only give space enough, and search enough, and the stones buried in the earth cry out to confirm each letter of Scripture. Old manuscripts, coins, and inscriptions are on the side of the Book, and against it there are nothing but theories, and the fact that many an event in history has no other record but that which the Book affords us. The Book has been of late in the furnace of criticism, but much of that furnace has grown cold from the fact that the criticism is beneath contempt.

There is not an error of any sort in the whole compass of them. These words come from Him who can make no mistake and who can have no wish to deceive His creatures. If I did not believe in the infallibility of the Book, I would rather be without it. If I am to judge the Book, it is no judge of me. If I am to sift it, like the heap on the threshing floor, and lay this aside and only accept that, according to my own judgment, then I have no guidance whatever, unless I have conceit enough to trust to my own heart. The new theory denies infallibility to the words of God but practically imputes it to the judgments of men; at least, this is all the infallibility they can get at. I protest that I will rather risk my soul with a guide inspired from heaven than with the differing leaders who arise from the earth at the call of "modern thought."

Again, this Book is pure in the sense of reliability; it has in its promises no admixture of failure. Mark this: no prediction of Scripture has failed. No promise that God has given will turn out to be mere verbiage. Take the promise as the Lord gave it, and you will find Him faithful to every jot and tittle of it. Some of us are not yet entitled to be called "old and greyheaded," but hitherto we have believed the promises of God and tested and tried them. And what is our verdict? I bear my solemn testimony that I have not found one word of the Lord fall to the ground.

The fulfilment of a promise has been delayed sometimes beyond the period which my impatience would have desired, but to the right instant the promise has been kept. You may lean your whole weight upon any one of the words of God, and they will bear you up. In your darkest hour, you may have no candle but a single promise, and yet that lone light shall make high noon of your midnight. Glory be to His name, the words of the Lord are without evil, without error, and without failure.

Furthermore, the text also speaks of the preciousness of God's words. David compares them to refined silver, and silver is a precious metal. In other places, he has likened these words to pure gold. The words of the Lord might have seemed comparable to paper money, but no, they are the metal itself. In the words of God, you have the solid money of truth; it is not fiction, but the substance of truth. God's words are as bullion. When you have them in the grip of faith, you have the substance of things hoped for. Faith finds in the promise of God the reality of what she looks for: the promise of God is as good as the performance itself. God's words, whether of doctrine, of practice, of comfort, are of solid metal to the man of God who knows how to put them in the purse of personal faith.

As we use silver in many articles within our houses, so do we use God's Word in daily life; it has a thousand uses. As silver is current coin of the merchant, so are the promises of God a currency both for heaven and earth. We deal with God by His promises, and so He deals with us. As men and women deck themselves with silver by way of ornament, so are the words of the Lord our jewels and our glory. The promises are things of beauty which are a joy forever. When we love the Word of God and keep it, the beauty of holiness is upon us. This is the true ornament of character and life, and we receive it as a love gift from the Bridegroom of our souls.

Furthermore, this text sets before us the permanence of the Lord's words. They are as silver that has passed through the hottest fires. Truly, the Word of God has for ages stood the fire—and fire applied in its fiercest form—that is to say, in that furnace that refiners regard as their last resort. If the devil could have destroyed the Bible, he would have brought up the hottest coals from the center of hell. He has not been able to destroy one single line.

Fire, according to the text, was applied in a skillful way: silver is placed in a crucible of earth, that the fire may get at it thoroughly. The refiner is quite sure to employ his heat in the best manner known to him, so as to melt away the dross. So have men with diabolical skill endeavored, by the most clever criticism, to destroy the words of God. Their object is not purification; they aim at consuming the divine testimony. Their labor is vain; for the sacred Book remains still what it always was: the pure words of the Lord. But some of our misconceptions of its meaning have happily perished in the fires.

The words of the Lord have been tried frequently. What more remains I cannot guess, but assuredly the processes have already been many and severe. It abides unchanged. The comfort of our fathers is our comfort. The words that cheered our youth are our support in age. These words of God are a firm foundation, and our eternal hopes are wisely built thereon. We cannot permit anyone to deprive us of this basis of hope. In the olden time, men were burned rather than cease to read their Bibles; we endure less brutal oppositions, but they are far more subtle and difficult to resist. Still, let us always abide by the everlasting words, for they will always abide by us.

The words of the Ever Blessed are unchanged and unchangeable. They are as silver without dross, which will continue from age to age. This we do believe, and in this we do rejoice. Nor is it a tax upon our faith to believe in the permanence of Holy Scripture, for these words were spoken by Him who is omniscient and knows everything; there can be in them no mistake. They were spoken by Him who is omnipotent and can do everything; His words will be carried out. Spoken by Him who is immutable, these words will never alter. The words God spoke thousands of years ago are true at this hour, for they come from Him who is the same yesterday, today, and forever. He who spoke these words is infallible, and therefore they are infallible. When did He ever err? Could He err, and yet be God?

THE TRIALS OF THE WORDS OF GOD

The words of God are said to be as silver, which has been tried in a furnace. The words of God have been tested by blasphemy, ridicule, persecution, criticism, and candid observation. I shall not attempt an oratorical flight while describing the historical tests of the precious metal of divine revelation, but I shall mention trials of a commonplace order that have come under my own notice, and probably under yours also. This may be more homely, but it will be more edifying.

In dealing with the sinner's obstinacy, we have tested the words of the Lord. There are men who cannot be convinced or persuaded; they doubt everything, and with closed teeth they resolve not to believe. They are encased in the armor of prejudice, and they cannot be wounded with the sharpest arrows of argument. What is to be done with the numerous clan who are related to Mr. Obstinate? You might as well argue with an express train: he runs on and will not stop, though a thousand should stand in his way. Will the words of God convince him?

There are some in this place today of whom I should have said, if I had known them before their conversion, that it was a vain task to preach the gospel to them because they so much loved sin, and so utterly despised the things of God. Strangely enough, they were among the first to receive the Word of God when they came under the sound of it. It came to them in its native majesty, in the power of the Holy Ghost. It spoke with a commanding tone to their inmost heart; it threw open the doors that had long been shut up and rusted on their hinges, and Jesus entered to save and reign. Brethren, we have only to have faith in God's Word and speak it out straight, and we shall see proud rebels yielding.

No mind is so desperately set on mischief, so resolutely opposed to Christ, that it cannot be made to bow before the power of the words of God. Oh, that we used more the naked sword of the Spirit! I am afraid we keep this two-edged sword in a scabbard and somewhat pride ourselves that the sheath is so elaborately adorned. What is the use of the sheath? The sword must be made bare, and we must fight with it without attempting to garnish it. Tell forth the words of God. Omit neither the terrors of Sinai nor the love notes of Calvary. Proclaim the Word with all fidelity, for the power of the highest and the most obstinate sinner out of hell can be laid low by its means. The Holy Spirit uses the Word of God: this is His one battering ram with which He casts down the strongholds of sin and self in those human hearts with which He effectually deals. The Word of God will bear the tests furnished by the hardness of the natural heart, and it will by its operations prove its divine origin.

When you have a man fairly broken down, who has but come part of the way, a new difficulty arises. Will the words of the Lord overcome the penitent's despair? The man is full of terror on account of sin, and hell has begun to burn within his bosom. You may talk to him lovingly, but his soul refuses to be comforted. Until you bring the words of the Lord to bear upon him, his "soul abhorred all manner of food" (Ps. 107:18). Tell him of a dying Savior; dwell on free grace and full pardon; speak of the reception of the prodigal son and of the Father's changeless love.

Attended by the power of the Spirit, these truths must bring light to those who sit in darkness. The worst forms of depression are cured when Holy Scripture is believed. Often have I been baffled when laboring with a soul convinced of sin and unable to see Jesus, but I have never had a doubt that in the end the words of the Lord would become a cup of consolation to the fainting heart. We may be baffled for a season, but with the words of the Lord as our weapons, despair will not defeat us. My Master's word is a great opener of prison doors; He has broken the gates of brass, and cut the bars of iron asunder.

That must be a wonderful word which, like a battle axe, smashes in the helmet of presumption and at the same time, like the finger of love, touches the tender wound of the bleeding and heals it in an instant. The words of the Lord, for breaking down or lifting up, are equally effectual.

In certain instances, the words of God are tried by the seeker's singularity. How frequently have persons told us that they were sure there was nobody like themselves in all the world! They were men up in a corner, strange fish, the like of which no sea could yield. Now, if these words be indeed of God, they will be able to touch every case. The words of God have been put to that test, and we are amazed at their universal adaptation. There is a text to meet every remarkable and out-of-the-way case. In certain instances, we have heard of an odd text, concerning which we could not before see why it was written, yet it has evidently a special fitness for a particular person to whom it has come with divine authority. The words of this Book are proved to be the words of God because they have an infinite adaptation to the varied minds the Lord has made.

Personally, when I have been in trouble, I have read the Bible until a text has seemed to stand out of the Book and salute me, saying, "I was written specially for you." It has looked to me as if the story must have been in the mind of the writer when he penned that passage; and so it was in the mind of that divine Author who is at the back of all these inspired pages. Thus have the words of the Lord stood the test of adaptation to the singularities of individual men.

We frequently meet with people of God who have tested the words of God in time of sore trouble. I appeal here to the experience of the people of God. You have lost a dear child. Was there not a word of the Lord to cheer you? You lost your property. Was there a passage in the Scriptures to meet the disaster? You have been slandered. Was there not a word to console you? You were very sick and depressed. Had not the Lord provided a comfort for you in that case? I will not multiply questions. The fact is that you never were high, but the Word of the Lord was up with you. And you never were low, but what the Scripture was down with you. No child of God was ever in any ditch, pit, cave, or abyss, but the words of God found him out. How often do the gracious promises lie in ambush to surprise us with their lovingkindness! I adore the infinity of God's goodness, as I see it mirrored in the glass of Scripture.

Again, the Word of God is tried and proved as a guide in perplexity. This book is an oracle to the simple-hearted man in mental, moral, and spiritual perplexity. Oh, that we used it more! Rest assured that you never will be in a labyrinth so complicated that this book, blessed of the Spirit, will not help you through. This is the compass for all mariners upon the sea of life. By its use you will know where lies the pole. Abide by the words of the Lord, and your way will be clear.

Beloved, the words of God endure another test: they preserve us in times of temptation. You can write a book that may help a man when he is tempted in a certain direction; will the same volume strengthen him when he is attracted in the opposite direction? Can you conceive a book that shall be a complete fence, encircling a man in all directions? Yet such is this Book. The devil himself cannot invent a temptation that is not met in these pages. It reaches the believer in every condition and position, and it preserves him from all evil. "How can a young man cleanse his way? By taking heed according to Your word" (Ps. 119:9).

Last on this point: this Book helps men to die. Believe me, it is no child's play to die! You and I will find ourselves in that solemn article, and then we shall need strong consolation. Nothing upon earth ever gives me so much establishment in the faith as to visit members of this church when they are about to die. It is very sad to see them wasting away or wracked with pain, but, nevertheless, the chief effect produced upon the visitor is gladsome rather than gloomy. Brethren, it is not hard to pass out of this world when we are resting on that old and sure gospel that I have preached to you these many years. I can both live and die on the eternal truths I have proclaimed to you, and this assurance makes me bold in preaching.

Now, if this inspired volume, with its wonderful record of the words of God, helps us in the trials of life, directs us in our daily paths, and enables us to weather the last great storm, surely it is precious beyond description, "like silver tried in a furnace of earth, purified seven times" (Ps. 12:6).

THE CLAIMS OF THE WORDS OF GOD

The claims of these words are many. First, they deserve to be studied. Beloved, may I urge upon you the constant searching of inspired Scripture? Here is the last new novel! What shall I do with it? Cast it on the ground. This sacred volume is the freshest of novels. It would be, to some of you, an entirely new book.

We have a society for providing the Bible for readers, but we greatly need readers for the Bible. I grieve that even to some who bear the Christian name, Holy Scripture is the least read book in their library. One said of a preacher the other day, "How does he keep up the congregation? Does he always give the people something new?" "Yes," said the other, "he gives them the gospel; and in these days, that is the newest thing out." It is truly so; the old, old gospel is always new. The modern doctrine is only new in name; it is, after all, nothing but a hash of stale heresies and moldy speculations. If God has spoken, listen! If the Lord has recorded His words in a Book, search its pages with a believing heart. If you do not accept it as God's inspired Word, I cannot invite you to pay any particular attention to it, but if you regard it as the Book of God, I charge you, study the Bible daily. Treat not the Eternal God with disrespect, but delight in His Word.

Do you read it? Then believe it. Oh, for an intense belief of every word that God has spoken! Do not hold it as a dead creed, but let it hold you as with an almighty hand. Have no controversy with any one of the Lord's words. Believe without a doubt. Until a doctrine becomes an absolute certainty to a man, he will never know its sweetness: truth has little influence upon the soul till it is fully believed.

Next, obey the Book. Do it freely, do it heartily, do it constantly. Err not from the commandment of God. May the Lord make you perfect in every good work, to do His will! You that are unconverted, may you obey that gospel word. Repentance and faith are at once the commands and the gifts of God; neglect them not.

Furthermore, these words of God are to be preserved. Give up no line of God's revelation. You may not know the particular importance of the text assailed, but it is not for you to assess the proportionate value of God's words: if the Lord has spoken, be prepared to die for what He has said. I have often wondered whether, according to the notions of some people, there is any truth for which it would be worthwhile for a man to go to the stake. I should say not, for we are not sure of anything, according to the modern notion. Would it be worthwhile dying for a doctrine that may not be true next week? Fresh discoveries may show that we have been the victims of an antiquated opinion. Had we not better wait and see what will turn up? It will be a pity to be burned too soon or to lie in prison for a dogma that will, in a few years, be superseded. Brethren, we cannot endure this shifty theology. May God send us a race of men who have backbones! Men who believe something and would die for what they believe. This Book deserves the sacrifice of our all for the maintenance of every line of it.

Believing and defending the Word of God, let us proclaim it. Go out this afternoon and speak in the street the words of this life. "Truth is mighty, and will prevail," they say; it will not prevail if it be not made known. The Bible itself works no wonders until its truths are published abroad. Tell it out among the heathen that the Lord reigns from the tree. Tell it out among the multitude that the Son of God has come to save the lost, and that whoever believes in Him shall have eternal life. Make all men know that "God so loved the world that He gave His only begotten Son, that whoever believes in Him should not perish but have everlasting life" (John 3:16). This thing was not done in a corner; keep it not a secret.

TITLE:
The Infallibility of Scripture

TEXT:
Isaiah 1:20

SUMMARY:
Although Isaiah spoke to the people of Israel, it was the Word of God. First, Spurgeon maintains this should be *our warrant for teaching scriptural truth*. We approach the task with awe and trembling, knowing the great responsibility. This gives us confidence and full assurance of our task. Second, Spurgeon shows in this text it is the *claim of God's Word upon your attention*. Because of His infinite majesty, every word He speaks is worthy of our attention. Third, Spurgeon shows that this gives *God's Word a very special character*. The Bible is like no other book, and it has been tested thoroughly. Because of this, it is *grounds for great alarm to many*. Finally, Spurgeon shows that *the Word is the reason and rest of our faith*.

NOTABLE QUOTES
"We repeat the Word as a child repeats his lesson."

"It is a living seed and the seed of life, and therefore we must diligently scatter it."

"Every word which God has given us in this Book claims our attention, because of the infinite majesty of Him that spoke it."

A sermon preached by Charles H. Spurgeon on March 11, 1888. *Metropolitan Tabernacle Pulpit*, vol. 34.

3

The Infallibility of Scripture

The mouth of the LORD has spoken.

ISAIAH 1:20

WHAT ISAIAH SAID was, therefore, spoken by the Lord. It was audibly the utterance of a man, but really it was the utterance of the Lord Himself. The lips that delivered the words were those of Isaiah, but yet it was the very truth that "the mouth of the LORD has spoken." All Scripture, being inspired of the Spirit, is spoken by the mouth of God. However this sacred Book may be treated nowadays, it was not treated contemptuously, nor negligently, nor questioningly by the Lord Jesus Christ, our Master and Lord. It is not your worry how He reverenced the written Word. The Spirit of God rested upon Him personally, without measure, and He could speak out of His own mind the revelation of God, and yet He continually quoted the law and the prophets and the Psalms. Always He treated the sacred writings with intense reverence, strongly in contrast with the irreverence of "modern thought."

I am sure, brethren, we cannot be wrong in imitating the example of our divine Lord in our reverence for that Scripture, which cannot be broken. If He, the anointed of the Spirit and able to speak Himself as God's mouth, yet quoted the sacred writings and used the holy Book in His teachings, how much more should we, who have no spirit of prophecy resting upon us and are not able to speak new revelations, come back to the law and to the testimony and value every single word that "the mouth of the Lord has spoken"?

The like valuation of the Word of the Lord is seen in our Lord's apostles. They treated the ancient Scriptures as supreme in authority and supported their statements with passages from Holy Writ. The utmost degree of deference and homage is paid to the Old Testament by the writers of the New. We never find an apostle raising a question about the degree of inspiration in this book or that. No disciple of Jesus questions the authority of the books of Moses or the prophets. If you want to cavil or suspect, you find no sympathy in the teaching of Jesus or any one of His apostles. The New Testament writers sit reverently down before the Old Testament and receive God's words as such, without any question whatever.

You and I belong to a school that will continue to do the same; let others adopt what behavior they please. As for us and for our house, this priceless Book shall remain the standard of our faith and the ground of our hope so long as we live. Others may choose what gods they will and follow what authorities they prefer, but as for us, the glorious Jehovah is our God, and we believe concerning each doctrine of the entire Bible, that "the mouth of the LORD has spoken."

OUR WARRANT FOR TEACHING
SCRIPTURAL TRUTH

We preach because "the mouth of the LORD has spoken." It would not be worth our while to speak what Isaiah had spoken if in it there was nothing more than Isaiah's thought; neither should we care to meditate hour after hour upon the writings of Paul if there was nothing more than Paul in them. We feel no imperative call to expound and to enforce what has been spoken by men. But since "the mouth of the LORD has spoken," it is woe unto us if we preach not the gospel! We come to you with "Thus saith the Lord," and we should have no justifiable motive for preaching our lives away if we have not this message.

The true preacher delivers his message with awe and trembling because "the mouth of the LORD has spoken." He bears the burden of the Lord and bows under it. Ours is no trifling theme but one that moves our whole soul. Martin Luther, who never feared the face of man, declared that when he stood up to preach he often felt his knees knock together under a sense of his great responsibility. Woe unto us if we dare to speak the Word of the Lord with less than our whole heart, soul, and strength. Woe unto us if we handle the Word as if it were an occasion for display!

If it were our own word, we might be studious of this grace

of oratory, but if it be God's Word, we cannot afford to think of ourselves. We are bound to speak it, "not with wisdom of words, lest the cross of Christ should be made of no effect" (1 Cor. 1:17). If we reverence the Word, it will not occur to us that we can improve upon it by our own skill in language.

Oh, it were far better to break stones on the road than to be a preacher, unless one had God's Holy Spirit to sustain him, for our charge is solemn and our burden is heavy. The heart and soul of the man who speaks for God will know no ease, for he hears in his ears that warning admonition: "If the watchman warn them not they shall perish; but their blood will I require at the watchman's hands."

If we were commissioned to repeat the language of a king, we should be bound to do it decorously lest the king suffer damage. But if we rehearse the revelation of God, a profound awe and a godly fear should take hold upon us lest we mar the message of God in telling it. No work is so important or honorable as the proclamation of the gospel of our Lord Jesus, and for that very reason, it is weighted with a responsibility so solemn that none may venture upon it lightly. We live under intense pressure who preach a gospel of which we can assuredly say, "The mouth of the Lord has spoken." We live rather in eternity than in time: we speak to you as though we saw the great white throne and the divine Judge before whom we must give our account not only for what we say but for how we say it.

Dear brethren, because the mouth of the Lord has spoken the truth of God, we therefore endeavor to preach it with absolute fidelity. We repeat the Word as a child repeats his lesson. It is not ours to correct the divine revelation but simply to echo it. Believing that "the mouth of the LORD has spoken," it is my duty to repeat it to you as correctly as I can after having heard it and felt it in my own soul. It is not mine to amend or adapt the gospel! Shall we attempt to improve upon what God has revealed? The Infinitely Wise—is He to be corrected by creatures of a day? Is the infallible revelation of the infallible Jehovah to be shaped, moderated, and toned down to the fashions and fancies of the hour? God forgive us if we have ever altered His Word unwittingly; wittingly we have not done so, nor will we.

His children sit at His feet and receive of His words, and then they rise up in the power of His Spirit to publish far and near the Word, which the Lord has given. "He that has my word, let him speak my word faithfully," is the Lord's injunction to us. If we could abide with the Father, according to our measure, after the manner of the Lord Jesus, and then come forth from communion with Him to tell what He has taught us in His Word, we should be accepted of the Lord as preachers and accepted also of His living people far more than if we were to dive into the profound depths of science or rise to the loftiest flights of rhetoric. What is the chaff to the wheat? What are man's discoveries to the teachings of the Lord?

Again, dear friends, as "the mouth of the LORD has spoken," we speak the divine truth with courage and full assurance. Modesty is a virtue, but hesitancy when we are speaking for the Lord is a great fault. If an ambassador sent by a great king to represent his majesty at a foreign court should forget his office and only think of himself, he might be so humble as to lower the dignity of his prince, so timid as to betray his country's honor. He is bound to remember not so much what he is in himself, but whom he represents; therefore, he must speak boldly and with the dignity of his office and the court he represents. We do not ask tolerance nor court applause. We preach Christ crucified, and we speak boldly as we ought to speak because it is God's Word and not our own. We are accused of dogmatism, but we are bound to dogmatize when we repeat that which the mouth of the Lord has spoken. We cannot use "ifs" and "buts," for we are dealing with God's "shalls" and "wills." If He says it is so, it is so, and there is an end of it. Controversy ceases when Jehovah speaks.

Those who fling aside our Master's authority may very well reject our testimony; we are content they should do so. But if we speak that which the mouth of the Lord has spoken, those who hear His Word and refuse it do so at their own peril. The wrong is done, not to the ambassador but to the King; not to our mouth but to the mouth of God, from whom the truth has proceeded.

We are urged to be charitable. We are charitable, but it is with our own money. We have no right to give away what is put into our trust and is not at our disposal. We are bold to declare with full assurance that which the Lord reveals. When we speak for the Lord against error, we do not soften our tones, but we speak thunderbolts. When we come across false science, we do not lower our flag—no, not for an hour. One word of God is worth more than libraries of human lore. "It is written" is the great gun that silences all the batteries of man's thought. They should speak courageously who speak in the name of the Lord, the God of Israel.

I will also add that because "the mouth of the LORD has spoken," we feel bound to speak His Word with diligence as often as we can and with perseverance as long as we live. Surely, it would be a blessed thing to die in the pulpit, spending one's last breath in acting as the Lord's mouth. Silent Sabbaths are fierce trials to true preachers. If we had common themes to speak about, we might leave the pulpit as a weary pleader quits the forum, but as "the mouth of the LORD has spoken," we feel His Word to be as fire in our bones, and we grow more weary with refraining than with testifying. The Word of the Lord is so precious that we must in the morning sow this blessed seed, and in the evening, we must not withhold our hands. It is a living seed and the seed of life, and therefore we must diligently scatter it.

Brethren, if we get a right apprehension concerning gospel truth, it will move us to tell it out with great ardor and zeal. We shall not drone the gospel to a slumbering handful. Many of you are not preachers, but you are teachers of the young, or in some other way you try to publish the Word of the Lord—do it, I pray you, with much fervor of Spirit. Enthusiasm should be conspicuous in every servant of the Lord. Let those who hear you know that you are all there, that you are not merely speaking from the lips outwardly but that from the depths of your soul, your very heart is welling up. The everlasting gospel is worth preaching, even if one stood on a burning bundle of sticks and addressed the crowd from a pulpit of flames. The truths revealed in Scripture are worth living for and dying for. I count myself thrice happy to bear reproach for the sake of the old faith. It is an honor of which I feel myself to be unworthy.

I cannot speak out my whole heart upon this theme that is so dear to me, but I would stir you all up to be instant in season and out of season in telling out the gospel message. Especially repeat such a word as this—"God so loved the world that He gave His only begotten Son, that whoever believes in Him should not perish but have everlasting life" (John 3:16). And this: "the one who comes to Me I will by no means cast out" (John 6:37). Tell it out boldly, tell it out in every place, tell it out to every creature, "for the mouth of the LORD has spoken." How can you keep back the heavenly news? Whisper it in the ear of the sick; shout it in the corner of the streets; write it on your tablets; send it forth from the press, but everywhere let this be your great motive and warrant: you preach the gospel because "the mouth of the LORD has spoken." Let nothing be silent that has a voice when the Lord has given the Word by His own dear Son.

THE CLAIM OF GOD'S WORD
UPON YOUR ATTENTION

Every word God has given us in this Book claims our attention because of the infinite majesty of Him who spoke it. I see before me a Parliament of kings and princes, sages and senators. I hear one after another of the gifted Chrysostoms pour forth eloquence like the "Golden-mouthed." They speak, and they speak well. Suddenly, there is a solemn hush. What a stillness! Who is now to speak? They are silent because God the Lord is about to lift up His voice. Is it not right that they should be so? What voice is like His voice? See that you refuse not Him who speaks.

Let it not be said of you that you went through this life, God speaking to you in His Book, and you refusing to hear! It matters very little whether you listen to me or not, but it matters a very great deal whether you listen to God or not. It is He who made you; in His hands your breath is; and if He speaks, I implore you, open your ear, and be not rebellious. There is an infinite majesty about every line of Scripture, but especially about that part of Scripture in which the Lord reveals Himself and His glorious plan of saving grace in the person of His dear Son, Jesus Christ. The cross of Christ has a great claim upon you. Hear what Jesus preaches from the tree. He says, "Incline your ear, and come to Me. Hear, and your soul shall live" (Isa. 55:3).

God's claim to be heard lies also in the condescension that led Him to speak to us. It was something for God to have made the world and bid us look at the work of His hands. Creation is a picture book for children. But for God to speak in the language of mortal men is still more marvelous, if you come to think of it. I wonder that God spoke by the prophets, but I admire still more that He should have written down His Word in black and white, in unmistakable language, that can be translated into all tongues, so that we may all see and read for ourselves what God the Lord has spoken to us and what, indeed, He continues to speak. O glorious Lord, do you speak to mortal man? Can there be any who neglect to hear you? If you are so full of lovingkindness and tenderness that you will stoop out of heaven to converse with your sinful creatures, none but those who are more brutal than the ox and the ass will turn a deaf ear to you!

God's Word has a claim, then, upon your attention because of its majesty and its condescension, but yet, further, it should win your ear because of its intrinsic importance. God never speaks vanity. No line of His writing treats of the frivolous themes of a day. That which may be forgotten in an hour is for mortal man, and not for the eternal God. When the Lord speaks, His speech is God-like, and its themes are worthy of one whose dwelling is infinity and eternity.

God does not play with you, man; will you trifle with Him? Will you treat Him as if He were altogether like you? God is in earnest when He speaks to you; will you not in earnest listen? He speaks to you of great things, which have to do with your soul and its destiny. Your eternal existence, your happiness or your misery hang on your treatment of what the mouth of the Lord has spoken. Concerning eternal realities, He speaks to you. I pray you, be not so unwise as to turn away your ear. Act not as if the Lord and His truth were nothing to you. Treat not the Word of the Lord as a secondary thing that might wait your leisure and receive attention when no other work was before you. Put all else aside, but hearken to your God.

Depend upon it, if "the mouth of the Lord has spoken," there is an urgent, pressing necessity. God breaks not silence to say what might as well have remained unsaid. His voice indicates great urgency. Today, if you will hear His voice, hear it, for He demands immediate attention. God does not speak without abundant reason, and, O my hearer, if He speaks to you by His

Word, I beseech you, believe that there must be overwhelming cause for it!

I know what Satan says: he tells you that you can do very well without listening to God's Word. I know what your carnal heart whispers: "Listen to the voice of business, and of pleasure; but listen not to God." But, oh! If the Holy Spirit shall teach your reason to be reasonable, and put your mind in mind of true wisdom, you will acknowledge that the first thing you must do is to heed your Maker. You can hear the voices of others another time; but your ear must hear God first, since He is first, and that which He speaks must be of first importance.

Without delay, make haste to keep His commandments. Without reserve, answer His call. When I stand in this pulpit to preach the gospel, I never feel that I may calmly invite you to attend to a subject that is one among many and may very properly be let alone for a time should your minds be already occupied. No. You may be dead before I again speak with you, and so I beg for immediate attention. I do not fear that I may be taking you off from other important business by entreating you to attend to that which the mouth of the Lord has spoken; for no business has any importance in it compared with this: this is the master theme of all. It is your soul, your own soul, your ever-existing soul that is concerned, and it is your God who is speaking to you. Do hear Him, I beseech you.

I am not asking a favor of you when I request you to hear the Word of the Lord; it is a debt to your Maker which you are bound to pay. Yea, it is, moreover, kindness to your own self. Even from a selfish point of view, I urge you to hear what the mouth of the Lord has spoken, for in His Word lies salvation. Hearken diligently to what your Maker, your Savior, your best friend, has to say to you.

THE CHARACTER OF GOD'S WORD

When we open this sacred Book and say of it that "the mouth of the LORD has spoken," then it gives to the teaching a special character.

In the Word of God, the teaching has unique dignity. This Book is inspired as no other book is inspired, and it is time that all Christians avowed this conviction. Where are we if our Bibles are gone? Where are we if we are taught to distrust them? If we are left in doubt as to which part is inspired and which is not, we are as badly off as if we had no Bible at all. I hold no theory of inspiration; I accept the inspiration of the Scriptures as a fact.

Those who thus view the Scriptures need not be ashamed of their company, for some of the best and most learned of men have been of the same mind. There are those on the side of God's Word whom you need not be ashamed of in the matter of intelligence and learning, and if it were not so, it should not discourage you when you remember that the Lord has hid these things from the wise and prudent and revealed them unto babes. We believe with the apostle that "the foolishness of God is wiser than men" (1 Cor. 1:25). It is better to believe what comes out of God's mouth and be called a fool than to believe what comes out of the mouth of philosophers and be esteemed wise.

There is also about that which the mouth of the Lord has spoken an absolute certainty. What man has said is unsubstantial, even when true. It is like grasping fog, there is nothing of it. But with God's Word, you have something to grip at, something to have and to hold. This is substance and reality. Though heaven and earth should pass away, yet not one jot or tittle of what God has spoken shall fail. We know that and feel at rest. God cannot be mistaken. God cannot lie. These are postulates which no one can dispute.

Again, if "the mouth of the LORD has spoken," we have in this utterance the special character of immutable fixedness. Once spoken by God, not only is it so now, but it always must be so. The Lord of Hosts has spoken, and who shall disannul it? The rock of God's Word does not shift like the quicksand of modern scientific theology. One would have need to read the morning papers and take in every new edition to know whereabout scientific theology now stands, for it is always chopping and changing. The only thing that is certain about the false science of this age is that it will be soon disproved. The great scientists live by killing those who went before them. They know nothing for certain, except that their predecessors were wrong.

We cannot adapt our religious belief to that which is more changeful than the moon. Try it who will. As for me, if "the mouth of the LORD has spoken," it is truth to me in this year of grace 1888. And if I stand among you a grey-headed old man somewhere in 1908, you will find me making no advance upon the divine ultimatum. Brothers and sisters, we hope to be together forever before the eternal throne, where bow the blazing seraphim, and even then we shall not be ashamed to avow that same truth which this day we feed upon from the hand of our God.

Here let me add that there is something unique about God's Word, because of the almighty power that attends it. "Where the word of a king is, there is power" (Eccl. 8:4); where the word of a God is, there is omnipotence. If we dealt more largely in God's own Word, we should see far greater results from our preaching. It is God's Word, not our comment on God's Word, that saves souls. Souls are slain by the sword, not by the scabbard, nor by the tassels which adorn the hilt of it. If God's Word be brought forward in its native simplicity, no one can stand against it. The adversaries of God must fail before the Word as chaff perishes in the fire. Oh, for wisdom to keep closer and closer to that which the mouth of the Lord has spoken!

A GROUND OF GREAT ALARM TO MANY

Shall I read you the whole verse? "'But if you refuse and rebel, you shall be devoured by the sword'; for the mouth of the LORD has spoken." Every threat that God has spoken, because He has spoken it, has a tremendous dread about it. Whether God threaten a man, a nation, or the whole class of the ungodly, if they are wise, they will feel a trembling take hold upon them. God has never yet spoken a threat that has fallen to the ground. When He told Pharaoh what He would do, He did it. When the Lord at any time sent His prophets to denounce judgments on the nations, He carried out those judgments. Ask travelers concerning Babylon and Nineveh and Edom and Moab and Bashan, and they will tell you of the heaps of ruins, which prove how the Lord carried out His warnings to the letter.

One of the most awful things recorded in history is the siege of Jerusalem. You have read it, I do not doubt, in Josephus or elsewhere. It was all foretold by the prophets, and their prophecies were fulfilled to the bitter end. You talk about God as being "love," and if you mean by this that He is not severe in the punishment of sin, I ask you what you make of the destruction of Jerusalem. Remember that the Jews were His chosen nation, and that the city of Jerusalem was the place where His temple had been glorified with His presence. Brethren, if you roam from Edom to Zion, and from Zion to Sidon, and from Sidon to Moab, you will find, amid ruined cities, the tokens that God's words of judgment are sure.

Depend on it, then, that when Jesus says, "These will go away into everlasting punishment" (Matt. 25:46), it will be so. When He says, "If you do not believe that I am He, you will die in your sins" (John 8:24), it will be so. The Lord never plays at frightening men. His Word is not an exaggeration to scare men with imaginary bugbears. There is emphatic truth in what the Lord says. He has always carried out His threatenings to the letter, and to the moment, He will continue to do so.

It is of no avail to sit down and draw inferences from the nature of God and to argue, "God is love, and therefore He will not execute the sentence upon the impenitent." He knows what He will do better than you can infer. He has not left us to inferences, for He has spoken pointedly and plainly. He says, "He who does not believe will be condemned" (Mark 16:16), and it will be so, "for the mouth of the LORD has spoken." Infer what you like from His nature, but if you draw an inference contrary to what He has spoken, you have inferred a lie, and you will find it so.

"Alas," says one, "I shudder at the severity of the divine sentence." Do you? It is well! The terrors of the Lord might well turn steel to wax. Let us remember that the gauge of truth is not our pleasure nor our terror. It is not my shuddering that can disprove what the mouth of the Lord has spoken. It may even be a proof of its truth. Did not all the prophets tremble at manifestations of God? One of the last of the anointed seers fell at the Lord's feet as dead. Yet all the shrinking of their nature was not used by them as an argument for doubt.

O my unconverted and unbelieving hearers, do remember that if you refuse Christ, and rush upon the keen edge of Jehovah's sword, your unbelief of eternal judgment will not alter it, nor save you from it. I know why you do not believe in the terrible threatenings. It is because you want to be easy in your sins. How can you believe that which condemns you? Ah! My friends, if you would believe it to be true and act accordingly, you would also find in that which the mouth of the Lord has spoken a way of escape from the wrath to come, for the Book is far more full of hope than of dread. This inspired volume flows with the milk of mercy and the honey of grace. It is not a doomsday book of wrath but a Testament of grace.

Yet, if you do not believe its loving warnings, nor regard its just sentences, they are true all the same. If you dare its thunders, if you trample on its promises, and even if you burn it in your rage, the holy Book still stands unaltered and unalterable, for "the mouth of the LORD has spoken." Therefore, I pray you, treat the sacred Scriptures with respect, and remember that "these are written that you may believe that Jesus is the Christ, the Son of God, and that believing you may have life in His name."

THE REASON AND REST OF OUR FAITH

"The mouth of the LORD has spoken" is the foundation of our confidence. There is forgiveness, for God has said it. Look, friend; you are saying, "I cannot believe that my sins can be washed away; I feel so unworthy." Yes, but "the mouth of the LORD has spoken." Believe over the head of your unworthiness. "Ah," says one, "I feel so weak I can neither think, nor pray, nor anything else, as I should." Is it not written, "When we were yet without strength, in due time Christ died for the ungodly"? "The mouth of the LORD has spoken it;" therefore, over the head of your inability, still believe it, for it must be so.

I think I hear some child of God saying, "God has said, 'I will never leave you, nor forsake you,' but I am in great trouble; all the circumstances of my life seem to contradict the promise." Yet, "the mouth of the LORD has spoken," and the promise must stand. "Trust in the LORD, and do good; dwell in the land, and feed on His faithfulness" (Ps. 37:3). Believe God in the teeth of circumstances. If you cannot see a way of escape or a means of help, yet still believe in the unseen God and in the truth of His presence. I think I have come to this pass with myself, at any rate for the time present, that when circumstances deny the promise, I believe it nonetheless.

When friends forsake me, and foes belie me, and my own spirit goes down below zero, and I am depressed almost to despair, I am resolved to hang onto the bare Word of the Lord and prove it to be in itself an all-sufficient stay and support. I will believe God against all the devils in hell, God against Ahithophel, and Judas, and Demas, and all the rest of the turncoats; yea, and God against my own evil heart. His purpose shall stand.

By-and-by, we shall come to die. The death-sweat shall gather on our brow, and perhaps our tongue will scarcely serve us. Oh that then, like the grand old German Emperor, we may say, "Mine eyes have seen your salvation." When we pass through the rivers, He will be with us, the floods shall not overflow us, "for the mouth of the LORD has spoken." When we walk through the valley of the shadow of death, we shall fear no evil, for He will be with us; His rod and His staff shall comfort us. Ah! What will it be to break loose from these bonds and rise into the glory? We shall soon see the King in His beauty and be ourselves glorified in His glory, for "the mouth of the LORD has spoken." "He who believes in Me has everlasting life" (John 6:47); therefore, a glad eternity is ours.

Brethren, we have not followed cunningly devised fables. We are resting on firm ground. We abide where heaven and earth are resting, where the whole universe depends, where even eternal things have their foundation: we rest on God Himself. If God shall fail us, we gloriously fail with the whole universe. But there is no fear; therefore, let us trust and not be afraid. His promise must stand, for "the mouth of the LORD has spoken." O Lord, it is enough.

TITLE:

Christ's Indwelling Word

TEXT:

Colossians 3:16

SUMMARY:

We can regard the whole of Scripture as the "word of Christ." Spurgeon first starts with *how we are to treat the Scriptures*. For the Scriptures to dwell in you, they must enter you. You must know it and believe it. When it has entered you, let it remain there and be your most familiar friend. Spurgeon then tells how you can *profit from the Word of Christ*. You must seek it, to profit yourself and others. It is also of profit to our relation to God Himself.

NOTABLE QUOTES

"The Bible reader is ever the Bible-lover, and the Bible searcher is the man who searches it more and more."

"Praying is the leaf of the rose, but praise is the rose itself, redolent with the richest perfume."

A sermon preached by Charles H. Spurgeon on April 10, 1881. *Metropolitan Tabernacle Pulpit*, vol. 46.

4

Christ's Indwelling Word

Let the word of Christ dwell in you richly in all
wisdom, teaching and admonishing one another
in psalms and hymns and spiritual songs, singing
with grace in your hearts to the Lord.

COLOSSIANS 3:16

THAT IS A VERY BEAUTIFUL NAME for Holy Scripture, I hardly remember to have met with it anywhere else: "Let *the word of Christ* dwell in you." Remember, dear friends, that Christ Himself is the Word of God, and recollect also that the Scriptures are the word of the Word. They are "the word of Christ." I think that they will be all the sweeter to you if you realize that they speak to you of Christ, that He is the sum and substance of them, that they direct you to Christ, in fact, as John says of his Gospel, that they were, "written that you may believe that Jesus is the Christ, the Son of God, and that believing you may have life in His name" (John 20:31).

Remember, also, that the Scriptures come to us from Christ. Every promise of this blessed Book is a promise of Christ, "for all the promises of God in Him are Yes, and in Him Amen, to the glory of God through us" (2 Cor. 1:20). Indeed, we may regard the whole of the sacred Scriptures, from the beginning of Genesis to the end of Revelation, as "the word of Christ."

HOW TO TREAT THE SCRIPTURES

In order that it may dwell in you, *it must first enter into you.* It is implied in our text that the apostle says, "Let the word of Christ enter into you." You must read it, or hear it, for unless you do, you will not know what is in it.

Yet there must be something more than the mere hearing or reading of it; for some hear the truth with one ear, but let it go away out of the other ear, and others are great readers, yet they seem to read only what is on the surface. The letter passes under their eye, but the deep spiritual meaning never enters into their heart. If you read a portion of Scripture every day, I commend you for doing so. If you make a practice of reading right through the Bible in a stated period, I commend you still more. Some I know read the Bible through every year, in due course.

This is well, but all this may be done, and yet "the word of Christ" may never have entered into the reader. You know how children sometimes learn their lessons. I am afraid that, at a great many schools, there is no true instruction. The scholars have simply to repeat their lessons without ever getting at the sense and meaning of them, and a week or two after, they have forgotten all that they were supposed to have learned. Do not let it be so with our knowledge of Scripture. Instead, "Let it dwell in you."

You must really know the spiritual meaning of it; you must believe it; you must live upon it; you must drink it in; you must let it soak into your innermost being as the dew saturated the fleece of Gideon. It is not enough to have a Bible on the shelf; it is infinitely better to have its truths stored up within your soul. It is a good thing to carry your Testament in your pocket, it is far better to carry its message in your heart.

How differently some people read the Bible from the way in which they read any other book! I have often noticed how people let novels get right into them, trash as they generally are, but when most people read the Bible, they appear to be anxious to get the unpleasant task finished. In some cases, they seem to think that they have performed a very proper action, but they have not been in the least affected by it, moved by it, stirred by it.

Yet, if there is any book that can thrill the soul, it is the Bible. If we read it aright, we shall lay our fingers among its wondrous harp strings and bring out from them matchless music. There is no book so fitted or so suited to us as the Bible is. There is no book that knows us so well, is so much at home with us, has so much power over us, if we will but give ourselves up to it.

Then, when it once gets into you, *let it remain there.* A person could not be said to dwell in a house even though he should enter into the most private part of it, if he only passed through it and went away. A man who dwells in a house abides, resides, remains, continues there. Oh, to have "the word of Christ" always dwelling inside of us—in the memory, never forgotten; in the heart, always loved; in the understanding, really grasped; with all the powers and passions of the mind fully submitted to its control! I love those dear Christian people who do not need to refer to the printed page when you speak to them about the things of God, for they have the truth in their hearts. They have a springing well within their souls at all times, and they have only to hear a scriptural theme started, and straightway they begin to speak of the things they have looked upon, and their hands have handled, of the Word of Life, because it dwells in them.

What is the good of merely external religion? I heard of some people who met together to pray about a certain matter, but they could not pray because the bishop had not sent the form of prayer they were to use on that occasion. I think that, if they were believers in the Lord Jesus Christ, they might have managed to speak to God without the necessity of having a written form to guide them. Yet there are many who fancy they cannot offer a proper prayer unless they have it in a book, and they cannot talk about the things of God, or they can say but very little about them, because they have not "the word of Christ" dwelling within them. O dear friends, let it be always in you, from morning to night, abiding as a constant visitor within your spirit—nay, not merely as a visitor, let it dwell with you.

Further, "let the word of Christ dwell in you" *so as to occupy your whole being.* If it dwells within you, let it take such entire possession of your being that it shall fill you. To push the truth of Christ up into a corner of your nature—to fill the major part of your being with other knowledge and other thought—is a poor way to treat "the word of Christ." It deserves the fullest attention of the best faculties that any man possesses.

The truth revealed by the Holy Ghost is so sublime that its poetry outsoars the eagle wing even of a Milton. It is a deep so profound that the plumb line of Sir Isaac Newton could never find the bottom of it. The greatest minds have been delighted to yield their highest faculties to its wondrous truths. Dear young friends, you who have only lately put on Christ, I beseech you not to let other books stand on the front shelf and the Bible lie behind. Do not, for the most part, read those other books, and only read small portions of Scripture now and then. Let it always have the chief place.

The most excellent of all sciences is the science of Christ crucified, and the Bible is the textbook for all who would learn it. If other forms of knowledge are useful, they are like the planets, but the knowledge of God as revealed in Christ Jesus is as the sun. Let this always be the center of your system of knowledge, and let all the rest that you know move in subordination and subjection to that first and best form of knowledge. Therefore, "let the word of Christ dwell in you" so as to occupy the whole of your being; let it be the resident, the occupant, the master and ruler of your entire nature.

Once more: "Let the word of Christ dwell in you," that is, *let it be your most familiar friend*. We know the people who live in our home, but we do not really know other people. It is living with people that lets you know what they are. In like manner, if you will live with "the word of Christ," especially if you will let it dwell in you and abide with you as a constant friend, you will get to know it better, and the better you know it, the more you will love it.

Ninety-nine times out of a hundred, if you meet with a man who finds fault with the Bible, you may be certain that he never read it. If he would but read it in the right spirit, he would be of another opinion. And if you find a professing Christian indifferent to his Bible, you may be sure that the very dust upon its cover will rise up in judgment against him.

The Bible reader is ever the Bible lover, and the Bible searcher is the man who searches it more and more. Various pursuits have a measure of fascination about them, but the study of God's Word is fascinating to the highest degree. The Bible is a book that has no bounds to it. Its thoughts are not as men's thoughts, a multitude of which may go to make up half an ounce; but any one of the thoughts of God can outweigh all the thoughts of men. This Book is not a book of pence, or a book of silver, or even a book of gold, but a book whose every leaf is of untold value. He shall be enriched indeed who lets "the word of Christ" richly dwell in him.

My dear friends, I should like you so to read the Bible that everybody in the Bible should seem to be a friend of yours. I should like you to feel as if you had talked with Abraham and conversed with David. I can truly say that there is hardly anybody in the world that I know so well as I know David. In making *The Treasury of David*, I have labored, year after year, in that rich field of inspiration, the book of Psalms, till I do assure you that David and I are quite familiar friends, and I think I know more about him than about any man I ever saw in my life. I seem to know the ins and outs of his constitution and experience, his grievous faults, and the graces of his spirit.

I want you to be on just such intimate terms with somebody or other in the Bible. Take the whole company of Bible saints home to your heart, let them live inside your soul. Let old Noah come in with his ark, if he likes, and let Daniel come in with his lions' den, if he pleases. And all the rest of the godly men and women of the olden time, take them all into your very nature and be on familiar terms with them, but be specially intimate with Him of whom they all speak, namely, Jesus Christ, your blessed Lord and Master.

As for the doctrines revealed in the Bible, you should have them at your fingers' ends. The great truths of the Word of God should be as familiar to you as a scholar makes his much-loved classics to be. So do you prize "the word of Christ"?

HOW TO PROFIT BY THE WORD OF CHRIST

First, *seek to profit by it yourself*: "Let the word of Christ dwell in you richly in all wisdom." Let it make you wise. The man who studies the Bible well will become a wise man. If God the Holy Ghost teaches him, I believe that he will become a wise man even in something more than a spiritual sense. I can truly say that, when I have met with men in whom "the word of Christ" has dwelled richly, I have often found them very shrewd even about common things. If you will take the Word of God for your guide, even in domestic and business matters, you will often manifest a shrewdness that, perhaps, may not be natural to you but that will come to you through "the word of Christ" dwelling in you richly in all wisdom. That, however, is only a small part of the profit which it will bring to you.

Do you want wisdom with which to master yourself? "Let the word of Christ dwell in you richly." Do you need something to cheer a naturally sinking spirit? "Let the word of Christ dwell in you richly." Do you wish for that that will calm an angry mind, a temper all too apt to be suddenly excited? "Let the word of Christ dwell in you richly." Are you in a calling where you are sorely tempted, and do you long to know how to be kept from falling into sin? "Let the word of Christ dwell in you richly." Is your position a very difficult one? Are you scarcely able to balance the claims of different relationships? "Let the word of Christ dwell in you richly." Are you expecting to have a time of intense strain and trial such as you have never experienced before? Prepare yourself for it by letting "the word of Christ dwell in you richly." It shall give you all manner of wisdom by which you shall be able to baffle even the subtlety of the old serpent himself.

The next way of using "the word of Christ" to profit is to *seek to profit others by it*: "Let the word of Christ dwell in you richly in all wisdom, teaching and admonishing one another in psalms and hymns and spiritual songs, singing with grace in your hearts to the Lord." We are to know the truth ourselves to be able to teach and admonish one another.

First, we are to seek the profit of our fellows by teaching one another. No one man can ever teach such a vast congregation as I have so as to give the separate instruction that is needed by each one; this work must be done by the members of the church themselves. "The word of Christ" must dwell in you, and then you must become a mutual instruction society. Every Christian should exercise the office of the pastorate according to his ability and his opportunity. Every member must look well not only to his own spiritual affairs but also to the well-being of others. What sweet and gracious instructions the older ones among you can give if you tell out your experience!

And if, in addition to relating your experience, you talk of the Scriptures that have been opened up to you, the passages in the Bible that have been applied to your heart by the Holy Spirit who inspired them, you will greatly instruct your fellow Christians. It is well to be busy for the Lord, but it is better still to be in communion with Him. Your who are deeply taught in the Scriptures should try to teach others also for their profit.

One way of teaching one another is mentioned in the text: "in psalms and hymns and spiritual songs." The apostle Paul thought that "psalms and hymns and spiritual songs" were to be used for instruction and admonition as well as for the praises of God. And to my mind, there is no teaching that is likely to be more useful than that which is accompanied by the right kind of singing. When I am preaching, I often find a verse of a hymn the very best thing I can quote, and I have not the shadow of a doubt that, frequently, a verse of sacred poetry has struck a man who has been altogether missed by the rest of the sermon. Think how compactly truth can be taught by means of "psalms and hymns and spiritual songs" and how likely it is to be remembered when the very measure and rhyme and rhythm help the memory to treasure up the message.

It is well to have truth put into the form of a verse that the memory may be able to lay hold of it and retain it. Do try, dear friends, to get so full of "the word of Christ" in all forms of it that you may run over with it. You know, it cannot come out of you if it is not first in you. If you do not get "the word of Christ" into you, you will not be instructive in your general conversation.

In addition to instruction, there is to be admonition. That is a very difficult thing to administer wisely. I have known a brother try to admonish another, and I have felt that he would have done better if he had left the task alone, for he has only caused irritation and resentment. But there is a gracious way of admonishing that cannot be too frequently practiced.

When I first began to preach, I am afraid that I used to say a great many strange things, but having, on a certain occasion, said something rather striking, and perhaps not quite wise, there was an excellent Christian man who wanted to set me right. He did not come and thrust himself upon me in a very solemn manner and provoke me to scoff at him. Neither did he say anything so as to irritate me, but finding my Bible lying about, he stuck a pin into it at the words, "Sound speech that cannot be condemned, that one who is an opponent may be ashamed, having nothing evil to say of you" (Titus 2:8).

When I was at home, I looked at that pin, and I looked at that text, and I said to myself, "Whose house was I in last?"

When I recollected, I said, "That is the man who stuck that pin in there, depend upon it." I never felt vexed with him; on the contrary, I was very grateful to him, and I always loved and admired him, and I thought, "Now, if he had spoken to me about what I had said, it is possible that he might have stuck the pin into me where I should not have liked it. But as he only stuck it into my Bible, it did not irritate me." You see, also, that I gratefully recollect the rebuke even to this day.

Sometimes, the best way to give an admonition will be by singing a psalm or a hymn. The clerks in the old meeting houses, when they used to be allowed to choose the hymns, have often taken away much of the evil effect of an erroneous sermon by their wise selection of the closing verses. Now and then, if you are discreet, you can quote an appropriate verse—as people say, "accidentally for the purpose"—and you can bring in a portion of a psalm that shall exactly say for you what you might have said in a blundering way. The dear brother who has done wrong will accept the rebuke without being enraged by it.

When you attempt to snuff the candle, do not put it out by your clumsiness, but take the golden snuffers—in the form of a verse of a psalm, or a hymn, or a spiritual song—and even while you sing it, you will be administering the admonition and the instruction that is your duty to give. What can we do unless you all look after one another? And how shall we ever get on unless, in addition to preaching, there shall be continual mutual instruction going on, wise and joyful and cheerful, and accepted in a kind, loving, and generous spirit? God fill you with "the word of Christ" that you may thus teach and admonish one another!

But, last, "the word of Christ" *is to profit us in our relation to God Himself*; for, after all, the main object of our singing must be the glory of God: "singing with grace in your hearts to the Lord." Oh, may "the word of Christ dwell in you" so richly that you shall bless God from morning to night! May you so overflow with holy thought and sacred knowledge that your whole being shall be a hymn of praise to the Most High, and your entire existence shall be a glorious hallelujah! I do not think that we any of us sufficiently value the divine ordinance of praise; neither do I think that we ever shall till "the word of Christ" has taken full possession of our souls.

You have been upstairs to pray, you say, and you have received no comfort from the exercise. Let me suggest that, the next time you go upstairs, you sing a psalm. How many times a day do you praise Him? I think you do get alone to pray, and you would be ashamed if you did not, once, twice, or three or even more times in the day, but how often do you praise God? Now, you know that you will not pray in heaven; there it will be all praise. Then do not neglect that necessary part of your education, which is to "begin the music here." Start at once praising the Lord.

Many of our doubts and fears would fly away if we praised God more, and many of our trials and troubles would altogether vanish if we began to sing of our mercies. Oftentimes depression of spirit that will not yield to a whole night of wrestling would yield to ten minutes of thanksgiving before God. Praying is the stalk of the wheat, but praise is the very ear of it. Praying is the leaf of the rose, but praise is the rose itself, redolent with the richest perfume.

Praise God, then, "in psalms and hymns and spiritual songs," and if you say you do not know how to do it, then "let the word of Christ dwell in you richly." It is a praise-begetting thing. Out of every book of Scripture will stream praise unto the Lord. Out of every promise will spring a sonnet. Out of every divine truth, enjoyed and lived upon, will rise a spiritual song. The whole revelation of God is the condensed essence of praise; you have only to give it a fitting opportunity, by setting it simmering on the fire of a grateful heart, and you shall find a sweet cloud of holy incense rising from it acceptable to the Most High. Therefore, beloved, be much with your Bibles, and let your Bibles be much with you, for your own profit, for the profit of others, and for the glory of God. So be it, for Christ's sake! Amen.

TITLE:

The Bible

TEXT:

Hosea 8:12

SUMMARY:

Spurgeon first looks at the *author*. He discusses the nature of human authors under divine inspiration. He highlights the Bible's authority and truthfulness. Spurgeon then moves onto the *subjects the Bible treats*. The last point Spurgeon makes is *the treatment the Bible receives in the world*. He exhorts the congregation to Bible reading and to recognize the prized place it has above all disciplines.

NOTABLE QUOTES

"Every verse in it has a solemn meaning, and if we have not found it out yet, we hope yet to do it."

"Come and drink out of this fair fount of knowledge and wisdom, and you shall find yourselves made wise unto salvation."

A sermon preached by Charles H. Spurgeon on March 18, 1855. *The New Park Street Pulpit*, vol. 1.

5

The Bible

"I have written for him the great things of My law, but they were considered a strange thing."

HOSEA 8:12

THIS IS GOD'S COMPLAINT against Ephraim. It is no mean proof of His goodness that He stoops to rebuke His erring creatures; it is a great argument of His gracious disposition that He bows His head to notice terrestrial affairs. He might, if He pleased, wrap Himself with night as with a garment; He might put the stars around His wrist for bracelets and bind the suns around His brow for a coronet; He might dwell alone, far, far above this world, up in the seventh heaven, and look down with calm and silent indifference upon all the doings of His creatures. He might do as the heathens supposed their Jove did, sit in perpetual silence, sometimes nodding His awful head to make the Fates move as He pleased but never taking thought of the little things of earth, disposing of them as beneath His notice, engrossed within His own being, swallowed up within Himself, living alone and retired. And I, as one of His creatures, might stand by night upon a mountaintop and look upon the silent stars, and say, "You are the eyes of God, but you look not down on me; your light is the gift of His omnipotence, but your rays are not smiles of love to me. God, the mighty Creator, has forgotten me; I am a despicable drop in the ocean of creation, a sear leaf in the forest of beings, an atom in the mountain of existence. He knows me not; I am alone, alone, alone."

But it is not so, beloved. Our God is of another order. He notices every one of us. There is not a sparrow or a worm but is found in His decrees. There is not a person upon whom His eye is not fixed. Our most secret acts are known to Him. Whatsoever we do, or bear, or suffer, the eye of God still rests upon us, and we are beneath His smile, for we are His people, or beneath His frown, for we have erred from Him.

We see from our text that God looks upon man, for He says of Ephraim, "I have written for him the great things of My law, but they were considered a strange thing." But see how when He observes the sin of man, He does not dash him away and spurn him with His foot; He does not shake him by the neck over the gulf of hell until his brain reels and then drop him forever. Rather, He comes down from heaven to plead with His creatures. He argues with them; He puts Himself, as it were, upon a level with the sinner, states His grievances, and pleads His claim.

I come here tonight in God's stead, my friends, to plead with you as God's ambassador, to charge many of you with a sin. The crime I charge you with is the sin of the text: God has written to you the great things of His law, but they have been unto you as a strange thing. It is concerning this blessed Book, the Bible, that I mean to speak tonight.

Concerning the Bible, I have three things to say tonight, and they are all in my text: first, its author, "*I* have written;" second, its subjects, the great things of God's law; and third, its common treatment, it has been accounted by most men a strange thing.

WHO IS THE AUTHOR?

The text says that it is God. "*I* have written for him the great things of My law." Here lies my Bible—who wrote it? This volume is the writing of the living God. Each letter was penned with an almighty finger; each word in it dropped from the everlasting lips; each sentence was dictated by the Holy Spirit.

Albeit that Moses was employed to write with his fiery pen, God guided that pen. It may be that David touched his harp and let sweet psalms of melody drop from his fingers, but God moved his hands over the living strings of his golden harp. It may be that Solomon sang canticles of love or gave forth words of consummate wisdom, but God directed his lips and made the preacher eloquent. If I follow the thundering Nahum when his horses plough the waters, or Habakkuk when he sees the tents of Cushan in affliction; if I read Malachi, when the earth is burning like an oven; if I turn to the smooth page of John, who tells of love, or the rugged, fiery chapters of Peter, who speaks of the fire devouring God's enemies; if I turn to Jude, who launches forth anathemas upon the foes of God, everywhere

I find God speaking. It is God's voice, not man's. The words are God's words, the words of the Eternal, the Invisible, the Almighty, the Lord of this earth. This Bible is God's Bible.

How do you know that God wrote the book? That is just what I shall not try to prove to you. I could, if I pleased, do a demonstration, for there are arguments enough. There are reasons enough, did I care to occupy your time in bringing them before you. But I shall do no such thing. I am a Christian minister, and you are Christians, or profess to be so, and there is never any necessity for Christian ministers to make a point of bringing forth infidel arguments in order to answer them. It is the greatest folly in the world. It is folly to bring forward these firebrands of hell even if we are well prepared to quench them. Let men of the world learn error of themselves; do not let us be propagators of their falsehoods.

But I shall neither plead nor argue this night. You profess to be Christian men or else you would not be here. Your profession may be lies, but still I suppose you all admit that this is the Word of God. A thought or two then upon it. "I have written for him the great things of My law."

First, my friends, stand over this volume and admire its authority. This is no common book. If these words were written by man, we might reject them, but oh, let me think the solemn thought—this Book is God's handwriting, these words are God's. Oh, Book of books! And were you written by my God? Then will I bow before you. You Book of vast authority, a proclamation from the Emperor of heaven; far be it from me to exercise my reason in contradicting you.

Reason! Your place is to stand and find out what this volume means, not to tell what this book ought to say. Come you, my reason, my intellect, sit you down and listen, for these words are the words of God. I do not know how to enlarge on this thought. If you could ever remember that this Bible was actually and really written by God! If you had been let into the secret chambers of heaven, if you had beheld God grasping His pen and writing down these letters, then surely you would respect them. But they are just as much God's handwriting as if you had seen God write them. This Bible is a book of authority; it is an authorized book, for God has written it. Oh, tremble, tremble, lest any of you despise it. Mark its authority, for it is the Word of God.

Then, since God wrote it, mark its truthfulness. If I had written it, there would be worms of critics who would at once swarm on it and cover it with their evil spawn. Had I written it, there would be men who would pull it to pieces at once. But this is the Word of God; come, critics, and find a flaw; examine it from its Genesis to its Revelation and find an error. This is a vein of pure gold unalloyed by quartz or any other substance. This is the judge that ends the strife where wit and reason fail. This is the book untainted by any error but is pure, unalloyed, perfect truth. Why? Because God wrote it.

Charge God with error if you please; tell Him that His book is not what it ought to be. I have heard men who would like to alter the Bible, and (I almost blush to say it) I have heard ministers alter God's Bible because they were afraid of it. I have heard men in prayer, instead of saying, "Make your calling and *election* sure," say, "Make your calling and *salvation* sure." Pity they were not born when God lived, that they might have taught God how to write. Oh, impudence beyond all bounds! Oh, full-blown self-conceit! Strange that there should be men so vile as to use the penknife of Jehoiakim to cut passages of the Word because they are unpalatable.

O you who dislike certain portions of the Holy Writ, rest assured that your taste is corrupt and that God will not stay for your little opinion. Your dislike is the very reason why God wrote it, because you ought not to be suited; you have no right to be pleased. God wrote what you do not like; He wrote the truth. Let us bend in reverence before it, for God inspired it. It is pure truth.

Yet once more, before we leave this point, let us stop and consider the merciful nature of God in having written us a Bible at all. He might have left us without it, to grope our dark way, as blind men seek the wall; He might have suffered us to wander on with the star of reason as our only guide. Supposing the light of nature to be sufficient, we had better have a little light from above too, and then we shall be sure to be right. Better have two lights than only one. The light of creation is a bright light. God may be seen in the stars; His name is written in gilt letters on the brow of night; you may discover His glory in the ocean waves, yea, in the trees of the field, but it is better to read it in two books than in one. You will find it here more clearly revealed, for He has written this book Himself, and He has given you the key to understand it, if you have the Holy Spirit. Ah, beloved, let us thank God for this Bible; let us love it. Let us count it more precious than much fine gold.

But let me say one thing before I pass on to the second point. If this be the Word of God, what will become of some of you who have not read it for the last month? Most people treat the Bible very politely. They have a small pocket volume, neatly bound; they put a white pocket-handkerchief around it and carry it to their places of worship. When they get home, they lay it up in a drawer till next Sunday morning, then it comes out again for a little bit of a treat and goes to chapel. That is all the poor Bible gets in the way of an airing. That is your style of entertaining this heavenly messenger. There is dust enough on some of your Bibles to write "damnation" with your fingers. There are some of you who have not turned over your Bibles for a long, long, long while, and what think you? I tell you blunt words, but true words. What will God say at last? When you shall come before Him, He shall say, "Did you read my Bible?"

"*No.*"

"I wrote you a letter of mercy; did you read it?"

"*No*"

"Rebel! I have sent you a letter inviting you to me; did you ever read it?"

"*Lord, I never broke the seal; I kept it shut up.*"

"Wretch!" says God. "Then you deserve hell, if I sent you a loving epistle, and you would not even break the seal; what shall I do unto you?"

Oh! Let it not be so with you. Be Bible readers; be Bible searchers.

THE SUBJECTS THE BIBLE TREATS

The Bible treats of great things, and of great things only. There is nothing in this Bible that is unimportant. Every verse in it has a solemn meaning, and if we have not found it out yet, we hope yet to do it. You have seen mummies wrapped round and round with folds of linen. Well, God's Bible is like that: it is a vast roll of white linen, woven in the loom of truth. You will have to continue unwinding it, roll after roll, before you get the real meaning of it from the very depth. When you have found, as you think, a part of the meaning, you will still need to keep on unwinding, unwinding, and all eternity you will be unwinding the words of this wondrous volume.

All things in the Bible are great. Some people think it does not matter what doctrines you believe or what church you attend. Well, I dislike Mrs. Bigotry above almost all people in the world, and I never give her any compliment or praise, but there is another woman I hate equally as much, and that is Mrs. Latitudinarian, a well-known character who has made the discovery that all of us are alike.

Now, I believe that a man may be saved in any church. Some have been saved in the church of Rome. I know, blessed be God, that multitudes are saved in the church of England. I think that all sections of Protestant Christians have a remnant according to the election of grace, and they had need to have, some of them, a little salt, for otherwise they would go to corruption. But when I say that, do you imagine that I think them all on a level? Are they all alike truthful? One sect says infant baptism is right, another says it is wrong, yet you say they are both right. I cannot see that. One teaches we are saved by free grace, another says that we are saved by free will, and yet you believe they are both right. I do not understand that. One says that God loves His people and never leaves off loving them; another says that He did not love His people before they loved Him. They may be both right in the main, but can they both be right when one says "Yes" and the other says "No"? It cannot be, sirs, that they are both right. But some say they differ upon nonessentials.

This text says, "I have written for him the *great* things of My law." There is nothing in God's Bible that is not great. Did ever any of you sit down to see which was the purest religion? "Oh," say you, "we never took the trouble. We just went where our father and mother went." Ah! That is a profound reason indeed. You went where your father and mother did. I thought you were sensible people; I didn't think you went where other people pulled you but went of your own selves. I love my parents above all that breathe, and the very thought that they believed a thing to be true helps me to think it is correct, but I have not followed them. I belong to a different denomination, and I thank God I do. I can receive them as Christian brethren and sisters, but I never thought that because they happened to be one thing I was to be the same. No such thing. God gave me brains, and I will use them; and if you have any intellect, use it too.

Never say it doesn't matter. It does matter. Whatever God has put here is of eminent importance; He would not have written a thing that was indifferent. But while all things in God's Word are important, *all are not equally important.* There are certain fundamental and vital truths which must be believed, or otherwise no man would be saved. If you want to know what you must believe if you would be saved, you will find the great things of God's law between these two covers; they are all contained here. As a sort of digest or summary of the great things of the law, I remember an old friend of mine once saying, "Ah! You preach the three R's, and God will always bless you: ruin, redemption, and regeneration." They contain the sum and substance of divinity.

I believe there is a better epitome in the five points of Calvinism: election according to the foreknowledge of God; the natural depravity and sinfulness of man; particular redemption by the blood of Christ; effectual calling by the power of the Spirit; and ultimate perseverance by the efforts of God's might. I think all those need to be believed in order to salvation.

God says, "I have written for him the great things of My law." Do you doubt their greatness? Do you think they are not worth your attention? Reflect a moment, man. Where are you standing now?

I recollect standing on a seashore once, upon a narrow neck of land, thoughtless that the tide might come up. The tide kept continually washing up on either side and wrapped in thoughts I still stood there until at last there was the greatest difficulty in getting on shore; the waves had washed between me and the shore. You and I stand each day on a narrow neck, and there is one wave coming up there; see how near it is to your foot, and lo, another follows at every tick of the clock: "our hearts . . . like muffled drums, are beating Funeral marches to the grave." We are always tending downwards to the grave each moment that we live. *This Book* tells me that if I am converted, when I die there is a heaven of joy and love to receive me; it tells me that angels' pinions shall be stretched, and I, borne by strong cherubic wings, shall out soar the lightning and mount beyond the stars, up to the throne of God, to dwell forever.

Oh! It makes the hot tear start from my eye; it makes my heart too big for this my body! Oh! That sweet scene beyond the clouds; sweet fields arrayed in living green, and rivers of delight. Are not these great things? But then, poor unregenerate soul, the Bible says if you are lost, you are lost forever; it tells you that if you die without Christ, without God, there is no hope for you, that there is a place without a gleam of hope where you shall read in burning letters, "You knew your duty, but you did it not." It tells you that you shall be driven from His presence with a "depart, you cursed." Are not these great things? Yes, sirs, as heaven is desirable, as hell is terrible, as time is short, as eternity is infinite, as the soul is precious, as pain is to be shunned, as heaven is to be sought, as God is eternal, and as His words are sure, these are great things, things you ought to listen to.

THE TREATMENT THE BIBLE
RECEIVES IN THIS WORLD

It is accounted a strange thing. What does that mean? In the first place, it means that it is very strange to some people, because they never read it. Ah! You know more about your ledgers than your Bible; you know more about your calendars than what God has written. Many of you will read a novel from beginning to end, and what have you got? A mouthful of froth when you have done. But you cannot read the Bible; that solid, lasting, substantial, and satisfying food goes uneaten, locked up in the cupboard of neglect while anything that man writes is greedily devoured.

"I have written for him the great things of My law, but they were considered a strange thing." You have never read it. I bring the broad charge against you. Perhaps, you say, I ought not to charge you with any such thing. I always think it better to have a worse opinion of you than too good of one. I charge you with this: you do not read your Bibles. Some of you never have read it through. I know I speak what your heart must say, is honest truth. You are not Bible readers. You say you have the Bible in your houses: do I think you are such heathens as not to have a Bible? But when did you read it last? How do you know that your spectacles, which you have lost, have not been there for the last three years? Many people have not turned over its pages for a long time, and God might say unto them, "I have written for him the great things of My law, but they were considered a strange thing."

Others there be who read the Bible, but when they read it, they say it is so horribly dry. That young man over there says it is a "bore." That is the word he uses. You do not love the Bible, do you? "No, there is nothing in it which is interesting." Ah! I thought so. But a little while ago *I* could not see anything in it. Do you know why? Blind men cannot see, can they? But when the Spirit touches the scales of the eyes, they fall off, and when He puts eye salve on, then the Bible becomes precious.

If you have tried God's Word and proved it, if it is precious to your souls, then you are Christians. But those persons who despise the Bible have "neither part nor portion in this matter" (Acts 8:21). If it is dry to you, you will be dry at last in hell. If you do not esteem it as better than your necessary food, there is no hope for you, for you lack the greatest evidence of your Christianity.

Alas! Alas! The worst case is to come. There are some people who hate the Bible as well as despise it. Is there such an one stepped in here? Some of you said, "Let us go and hear what the young preacher has to say to us." This is what he has to say to you: "Behold you despisers, marvel and perish!" This is what he has to say to you: "The wicked shall be turned into hell, and all the nations that forget God" (Ps. 9:17). But more: he tells you tonight that if you are saved, you must find salvation here. Therefore, despise not the Bible, but search it, read it, and come unto it. Rest assured, O scorner, that your laughs cannot alter truth; your jests cannot avert your inevitable doom. In vain you mock, for eternal verities are mightier than your sophistries. Nor can your smart sayings alter the divine truth of a single word of this volume of Revelation. Oh! Why do you quarrel with your best friend and ill-treat your only refuge? There yet remains hope even for the scorner: hope in a Savior's veins, hope in the Father's mercy, hope in the Holy Spirit's omnipotent agency.

My friend, the philosopher, says it may be very well for me to urge people to read the Bible, but he thinks there are a great many sciences far more interesting and useful than theology.

Extremely obliged to you for your opinion, sir. What science do you mean? The science of dissecting beetles, and arranging butterflies? "No," you say, "certainly not." The science, then, of arranging stones, and telling us of the strata of the earth? "No, not exactly that." Which science then? "Oh, all sciences," say you, "are better than the science of the Bible." Ah! Sir, that is your opinion, and it is because you are far from God that you say so.

But the science of Jesus Christ is the most excellent of sciences. Let no one turn away from the Bible because it is not a book of learning and wisdom. It is. Would you know astronomy? It is here: it tells you of the Sun of Righteousness and the Star of Bethlehem. Would you know botany? It is here: it tells you of the plant of renown—the Lily of the Valley and the Rose of Sharon. Would you know geology and mineralogy? You shall learn it here: for you may read of the Rock of Ages and the white stone with a name graven thereon, which no man knows, saving he who receives it. Would you study history? Here is the most ancient of all the records of the history of the human race. Whatever your science is, come and bend over this Book; your science is here. Come and drink out of this fair fount of knowledge and wisdom, and you shall find yourselves made wise unto salvation. Wise and foolish, babes and men, grey-headed sires, youths and maidens: I speak to you, I plead with you, I beg of you, respect your Bibles and search them out, for in them you have eternal life, and these testify of Christ.

Let us go home and practice what we have heard. If you will recollect to go home and read your Bibles, I shall have said enough. And may God, in His infinite mercy, when you read your Bibles, pour into your soul the illuminating rays of the Sun of Righteousness by the agency of the ever-adorable Spirit. Then you will read to your profit and to your soul's salvation.

TITLE:

The Warnings and Rewards of the Word of God

TEXT:

Psalm 19:11

SUMMARY:

Spurgeon begins this sermon with the idea that the Word *keeps us*. God's Word is our keeper; it warns us to see how sinful sin is and reminds us of our duty to God. Spurgeon then speaks of *our keeping the Word of God*. We should have reverent esteem for the Word and keep it. We should know it and be able to defend it. In keeping the Word, we grow in conformity to Christ. Our reward is holiness.

NOTABLE QUOTES

"You have mines of treasure if you have the Word of God dwelling richly in your heart."

"God's Word is our keeper, the watcher of our souls, and when a danger is approaching, it rings the alarm."

A sermon preached by Charles H. Spurgeon on March 16, 1890. *Metropolitan Tabernacle Pulpit*, vol. 36.

6

The Warnings and Rewards of the Word of God

Moreover by them Your servant is warned, and in keeping them there is great reward.

PSALM 19:11

THIS IS THE DECLARATION of one of God's servants: "by them Your servant is warned." Only for men made obedient by divine grace is this passage written. My hearer, are you God's servant? Let us begin with that question. Remember that if you are not God's servant, you are the bondslave of sin, and the wages of sin is death.

The psalmist has compared the Word of God to the sun. The sun in the heavens is everything to the natural world, and the Word of God in the heart is everything in the spiritual world. The world would be dark and dead and fruitless without the sun; and what would the mind of the Christian be without the illuminating influence of the Word of God? If you despise Holy Scripture, you are like one who despises the sun. It would seem that you are blind, and worse than blind; for even those without sight enjoy the warmth of the sun.

How depraved are you if you can perceive no heavenly luster about the Book of God! The Word of the Lord makes our day, it makes our spring, it makes our summer, it prepares and ripens all our fruit. Without the Word of God, we should be in the outer darkness of spiritual death. I have not time this morning to sum up the blessings showered upon us through the sun's light, heat, and other influences. So it is with the perfect law of the Lord: when it comes in the power of the Spirit of God upon the soul, it brings unnumbered blessings, blessings more than we ourselves are able to discern.

The revelation of God enriches the mind with knowledge, the heart with comfort, the life with holiness, the whole man with divine strength. He who studies, understands, and appropriates the statutes of the Lord is rich in the truest sense—rich in holiness for this life and rich in preparedness for the life to come. You have mines of treasure if you have the Word of God dwelling richly in your heart. But in the sacred Book, we find not only an enrichment of gold laid up but a present abundance of sweetness to be now enjoyed. He who lives upon God's Word tastes the honey of life, a sweetness far superior to honey, for honey satiates, though it never satisfies, it cloys and never contents. The more you have of divine teaching, the more you will wish to have and the more will you be capable of enjoying. He who loves the inspired Book shall have wealth for his mind and sweetness for his heart.

David is mainly aiming at the practical, so, having introduced the sun as the symbol of God's Word because of its pleasurable influence, he adds, "Moreover by them Your servant is warned, and in keeping them there is great reward."

THE WORD KEEPS US

We are in an enemy's country and always in danger; we are most in peril when we think ourselves most secure. You will find in the histories of the Bible that the most crushing defeats have fallen upon armies on a sudden, when they were off their guard. The army of Christ has need always to set its pickets and appoint its sentinels, lest the adversary take us unawares. We can never tell when we are likely to be assailed; we shall be wise to assume that we are always surrounded by enemies. God's Word is our keeper, the watcher of our souls, and when a danger is approaching, it rings the alarm. The different parts of Scripture—the statutes, the doctrines, the ordinances, the promises, the precepts—all of these act like pickets to the army and arouse the Lord's soldiers to resist sudden assaults: "By them Your servant is warned."

In what ways does God's Word warn us? In many forms it thus operates. I would say, first of all, by pointing out sin and describing its nature and danger. We have here the mind of the Lord as to moral conduct, and so we are not left to guesswork. We know by unerring teaching what it is that the Lord abhors.

Those Ten Commandments are like lanterns set around an opening in the street. God only forbids that which would injure us, and He only commands that which will be for our lasting good. Spread out before you the law of God, and you may say of it as you read it, "By these commandments Your servant is warned." In my walks, I see notices bearing the words TRESPASSERS BEWARE! and I am kept from wandering.

It is well to be acquainted not only with the letter of the law of the Lord but with the spirit of it. Numberless sins are condemned by the Ten Commandments; truly we may say of the law of God, "Your commandment is exceedingly broad" (Ps. 119:96). All of these are foghorns warning us of dangers that may shipwreck our souls.

Studying the Word of God, we are made to see that sin is exceeding sinful since it dishonors God, makes us enemies to our best friend, and drives us madly to destroy our own souls. Sin, according to God's Word, is murderous: it slew the Savior of men. Wherever sin comes, death follows it. Sin may bear pleasure in its face, but it has ruin at its heel. Eternal destruction is the finishing of the work of sin. God's Word is plain and explicit about these grave facts. It forbids our trifling even with the appearance of evil. It warns us against sins of thought and temper as well as against transgressions of speech and act.

He who is graciously familiar with his Bible will be preserved from those pitfalls into which so many have rushed in their careless contempt of God's Word and holy commandment. A precept of Scripture is like a lighthouse upon a quicksand or a rock; it quietly bids the wise helmsman to steer his vessel another way. The whole coast of life is guarded by these protecting lights, and he who will take note of them may make safe navigation. But remember, it is one thing for the Scripture to give warning and another for us to take it; and if we do not take warning, we cannot say, "By them Your servant is warned." Oh, that our hearts may be in such a state that a hint from the Word may set us on our watch against evil!

Next, the Word of God warns us by reminding us of our duties. We are not only taught negatively what we should not do but positively what we ought to do, and thus we are warned against sins of omission. I wish that professors who are neglectful of many points in the Savior's example would study His character more, marking down the points wherein they come short of it. If we were to read the lives of holy men recorded in Scripture and notice wherein we fail to be like them, it might do us much service. Truly, Lord, your servants would be profitably warned if we oftener enquired, "Lord, what would you have me to do?" Turning over these sacred pages, we remark a choice blessing coming upon a man of God in connection with a certain virtue, then are we warned to cultivate that virtue if we would have that blessing. The Lord does not pay us for our work as though we were hirelings and our labor meritorious, but still, according to His grace, He rewards His faithful servants and so encourages them diligently to obey. Every Bible precept should be an arrow aimed at the heart of our carelessness and forgetfulness. Then should we often say with David, "By them Your servant is warned." Like our Lord in His youth, we must be about our Father's business, and we must continue therein till, like Him, we can say, "I have finished the work which You have given Me to do" (John 17:4).

The Word of God also warns us of our weakness in those duties it commands and of our tendency to fall into those sins it forbids. It sets before us a noble example, but it bids us remember that only by divine power can we follow it. It spreads before us a program of perfect holiness, but it does not flatter us with the notion that by our own strength we can carry it out. It humbles us by showing that we cannot even pray as we ought without the Spirit's teaching nor so much as think a good thought without His aid. Scripture is continually warning us of the deceitfulness of our hearts and of the tendency of sin to advance from one stage of evil to another.

Scripture shows us our spiritual inability, apart from the Divine Spirit, and greatly do we need warnings in this way, for we are given to be self-sufficient. Pride will shoot forth with the very least encouragement. How soon we think ourselves near perfection when indeed we are near a fall! We are apt to sit down and imagine that we have won the race, whereas we have not yet traversed one-half of the way. The Word of God continually checks our carnal confidence and disturbs our self-satisfaction. It bears constant protest against our imagining that we have already attained when we are as yet only babes in grace. It shows us where our great strength lies, but it calls us off from all trust in our own past experience, or firmness of character, or strength of determination, or depth of sanctification to lean alone upon heavenly grace, which we must receive hour by hour. If we give way to pride, it is against the admonitions of the divine statutes.

So does the Word continually warn us against the temptations in the world in which we live. Read its story from the first day of Adam's fall to the last chapter of its record, and you shall find it continually representing the world as a place of trial for the heir of heaven. Christ seems praying over us every day as we read the Scripture, "I do not pray that You should take them out of the world, but that You should keep them from the evil one" (John 17:15).

If you fancy that your position in life puts you beyond temptation, you are sadly deluded. Poverty has its evil side, and riches are full of snares. Even in a Christian family, we may be seduced into great sin. There is no place under heaven where the arrows of temptation cannot reach us.

With this also comes persecution, for because we are not of the world, the world hates us. "In the world you will have tribulation" (John 16:33) is a sure prophecy. If you meet with no persecution, you should remember that the smiles of the world are even more dangerous than its frowns. Beware of prosperity! Thank God if you have the world's wealth, but hold it tenderly, and watch over your heart carefully, lest you bow before the golden calf. Adversity has less power to harm than prosperity.

We are continually warned to put on the whole armor of God and not to lay aside the shield of faith for a moment. We are urged to watch at all times and to pray without ceasing, for in the most quiet life, in the most pious company, and in the regular work of the day, dangers are lurking. Where we think we may be very much at ease, lying down as on a bank of flowers, we are most likely to be stung by the deadly serpent.

Here, let me add, we are warned repeatedly against the temptations of Satan. Certain theologians nowadays do not believe in the existence of Satan. Those who are most deluded by him are the loudest in repudiating all faith in his existence. Any man who has had experience of his temptations knows that there is a certain mysterious personage, invisible but almost invincible, who goes about seeking whom he may devour. He has a power far beyond that which is human and a cunning that is equal to that of a thousand of the cleverest of men. He will endeavor to influence our minds in a way contrary to their true intent, to turn our thoughts in directions we abhor, to suggest questions about truths of which we are certain, and even blasphemies against Him who, in our heart of hearts, we worship lovingly.

The power of Satan in a Christian man's life is a force with which he must reckon, or he may fail through ignorance. Some especially have had sore conflict with this evil one, and certain tried ones are scarcely a day without being tormented either by the howling of this dog or else by his snapping at their heels. He cannot possess us as he possesses many of the ungodly, but he worries whom he can't devour with a malicious joy. Whatever "modern thought" ministers may have to say about him, the inspired Scripture does not leave us ignorant of his devices but sets us on our guard against his terrible power, bidding us pray, "Do not lead us into temptation, but deliver us from the evil one" (Matt. 6:13).

The temptations of the world and of the flesh are more upon our level than the assaults of Satan. He is the prince of the evil forces, and his attacks are so mysterious, so cunningly adapted to our infirmities, and so ingeniously adjusted to our circumstances that unless the Lord the Holy Spirit shall daily cover us with His broad shield of grace, we shall be in the utmost jeopardy. O Lord, by these words of Yours is Your servant warned to resist the enemy and escape his wiles! Glory be to Your loving care!

The teachings of the Lord also warn us to expect trial. The Bible never promises the true believer an easy life. Rather, it assures him that he is born to trouble as the sparks fly upward. There is no soaring to heaven on the wings of luxurious ease; we must painfully plod along the pilgrim way. We see on the page of inspiration that we cannot be crowned without warfare, nor honored without suffering. Jesus went to heaven by a rough road, and we must follow Him. Every believer in the cross must bear the cross.

Those happiest of men, of whom it could be said that God had set a hedge about them and all that they had, these, in due course, had to take their turn at the whipping post and smart under the scourge. Even Job, that perfect and upright man, was not without his troubles. Beloved, expect to be tried, and when the trial comes, count it not a strange thing. Your sea will be rough, like that which tossed your Lord. Your way will be hot and weary, like that which your Master trod. The world is a wilderness to you, as it was to Him. "Both thorns and thistles it shall bring forth for you" (Gen. 3:18). Seek not to build your mansion here, for a voice cries to you out of the Word, "This is not your rest: because it is polluted" (Mic. 2:10 KJV). Therefore, beloved, you are forewarned that you may be forearmed.

God's Word also warns us by prophesying to us of things to come. I cannot enter just now into what is a very interesting point of experience, namely, the singular fact that the Bible is used of God to warn individuals of events about to occur to them. The Book is full of prophecies for nations, but at times, it becomes prophetic to individual believers. Have you never had impressed upon your mind a passage of Scripture that has followed you for hours, and even days, and you could not tell why, till an event has happened which has so exactly tallied with that Scripture that you could not but remark it as having prepared you for the circumstance? Will not your morning reading sometimes forestall the sorrow or the duty of the day? Have you not often found that if you read the Bible consecutively, somehow or other, the passage that comes in due course will prove to be as truly a lesson for the day, as if it had been written on purpose to meet your case? I am far from being superstitious, or wishful to encourage faith in mere impressions, but I cannot shut my eyes to facts which have happened to myself. I know that I have received, through this Book of God, messages to my heart that have come with peculiar power and suitability so that I have been compelled to say, with emphasis, "Moreover by them Your servant is warned."

But the Bible warns us all of certain great events, especially of the second advent of the Lord and the coming judgment. It does not clearly tell us when our Lord will appear, but it warns us that, to the unprepared, He will come as a thief in the night. It warns us of the general judgment and of the day when all men shall live again and stand before the great white throne. It warns us of the day when every secret shall be revealed and when every man shall receive for the things that he has done in his body, whether it be good or evil. "By them Your servant is warned."

If I live like one of yonder cattle in the immediate present, if I have no use for the future that is hurrying on, if my soul never places herself in vision before the judgment seat of Christ, if I never foresee the day when heaven and earth, before the presence of the great Judge, shall flee away, why then, I cannot be a diligent reader of the Word of God. If I search the Scriptures, I shall be called to walk in the light of the last day and shall be made to gird up my loins to face the dread account. Oh, that we might all be warned to be ready, that we may give in our account with joy! Oh, that we may so take the warnings of Holy Writ as to be ready for death, ready for judgment, and ready for that final sentence that can never be reversed! If we were truly wise, these warnings would put salt into our lives and preserve them from the corruption in the world.

Beloved, I trust that every one of us who knows the Lord will use His holy Book as the constant guard of his life. Let it be like a fog signal to you going off in warning when the road is hidden by a cloud. Let it be like the red lamp on the railway, suggesting you come to a stand, for the road is dangerous. Let it be like a dog at night, waking you from sleep because a robber is breaking in. Or as the watch on board a ship who shouts aloud, "Breakers ahead!" O precious Book, ring the alarm bell in my ear and compel me to flee from the wrath to come. Day and night, wherever I may be, may a word from the oracle of God sound in my ears and keep me from sleeping on the brink of the abyss! May no enemy be able to steal upon us when sleeping in false security, for it is high time that we awake out of sleep. This Book tells us so.

WE KEEP THE WORD

"In keeping them there is great reward." What is meant by keeping the testimonies of God's Word? You know right well that it will not suffice to have the holy Book in your houses, to lie upon the table so that visitors may see that you have a family Bible. Nor is it enough to place it on the bookshelf where the dust may thickly cover it because it is never used. That is not keeping the Bible but burying it. It does not warn you, for you smother it; you do not keep it, for you dishonor it by neglect. You must have a reverent esteem for it, and a growing familiarity with it, if you would keep it. "Let the word of Christ dwell in you richly" (Col. 3:16).

To keep the Word of God is, first of all, earnestly to study it so as to become acquainted with its contents. Know your Bible from beginning to end. I am afraid there is but little Bible searching nowadays. If the Word of God had been diligently studied, there would not have been so general a departure from its teachings. Bible-reading people seldom go off to modern theology. Those who feed upon the Word of God enjoy it too much to give it up. Comparing spiritual things with spiritual, they learn to prize all revealed truth, and they hold fast the faith once for all delivered to the saints. Dear young people, if you never read a single book of romance, you will lose nothing, but if you do not read your Bibles, you will lose everything. This is the age of fiction, and hence the age of speculation and error. Leave fiction and give yourself wholly to the truth. The Bible is the thesaurus of heavenly knowledge, the encyclopedia of divine science: read, mark, learn, and inwardly digest the same, and then you will be keeping the sayings of God.

But we cannot keep them without going further than this: we must be zealous in their defense. May it be said of each one of us, "You have kept My Word." When you find others denying God's truth, hold you the faster to it. When they argue against it, be prepared to give a reason for the hope that is in you with meekness and fear. It is not an easy task to stand fast in the faith today, for the current that runs toward unbelief is strong as a torrent, and many have been taken off their feet by it and are being carried down to the cataracts of error.

May God help you to say with the pilgrims in Vanity Fair, "We buy the truth!" Buy it at any price, and sell it at no price. It ought to be dearer than life, for it was so to the martyrs of our own country and to the Covenanters of Scotland, in whose steps we would tread. They cared little whether their heads were struck off or no, but they cared everything for King Jesus and the statutes of His Word. Beloved, happy in the end will that man be who for a while has suffered contempt, and misrepresentation, and separation from his brethren because of fidelity to the truth of God! Come what may, he who sides with truth will be no loser in the end.

But this is not all; we must go much further. There must be a careful observance of the law of the Lord. We cannot be said to keep God's Word if we never carry it out in our own lives. If we know the commandments but do not obey them, we increase our sin. If we understand the truth and talk about it but are slow to live according to it, what will become of us? This is not to keep God's Word but to hold the truth of God in unrighteousness. This may, in some cases, be a presumptuous sin. When your knowledge far exceeds your practice, take heed lest you be guilty of sinning willfully. We must keep the Word of God in the sense in which our Lord used the word when He said, "If you love Me, keep My commandments" (John 14:15).

Once more, even this is not enough. We are to keep the truth of God not only by reverent study of it, by zealous propagation of it, by careful observance of it, but also by an inward cleaving to it in love and a cherishing of it in our heart of hearts. What you believe you must also love if you are to keep it. If it comes to you in the power of God, it may humble you, it may chasten you, it may refine you as with fire, but you will love it as your life. It will be as music to your ear, as honey to your palate, as gold to your purse, as heaven to your soul. Let your very self be knit to the faithful Word. As newborn babes desire the unadulterated milk, so do you desire the teachings of the Spirit, that you may grow thereby. Every word of God must be bread to us, after which we hunger, and with which we are satisfied. We must love it even more than our necessary food. For that which God has spoken, we must have an ever-burning, fervent love that no floods of destructive criticism can quench or even dampen.

But now the text says, "in keeping them there is great reward." Here you must have patience with me while I set out the great reward that comes to obedient believers. There are many rewards, and the first is great quiet of mind. "Great peace have those who love Your law, and nothing causes them to stumble" (Ps. 119:165). When a man has done what God bids him do, his conscience is at peace. I can bear anybody to be my foe rather than my conscience. When a man's own conscience is his foe, where can he run for shelter? Conscience smites home, and the wound is deep.

But when a man can conscientiously say, "I did the right thing; I held the truth; I honored my God," then the censures of other men go for little. In such a case, you have no trouble about the consequences of your action, for if any bad consequence should follow, the responsibility would not lie with you. You did what you were told. Having done what God Himself commanded you, the consequences are with your Lord and not with you. If the heavens were likely to fall, it would not be our duty to shore them up with a lie. If the whole church of God threatened to go to pieces, it would be no business of ours to bind it up by an unhallowed compromise. If you should fail to achieve success in life, as men call success, that is no fault of yours if you cannot succeed without being dishonest. It will be a greater success to be honest and to be poor than to grow rich through trickery. If, through grace, you have done the will of God, your peace shall be like a river and your righteousness like the waves of the sea. Can you think of a greater reward than this? I cannot. A quiet conscience is a little heaven.

To do right is better than to prosper. A heart sound in the truth is greater riches than a houseful of silver and gold. There is more honor in being defeated in the truth than in a thousand victories gained by policy and falsehood. Though fame should give you the monopoly of her brazen trumpet for the next ten centuries, she could not honor you so much as you will be honored by following right and truth, even though your integrity be unknown to men. In keeping the Word of the Lord there is great reward, even if it bring no reward. The approbation of God is more than the admiration of nations. Verily this is great reward.

The next great reward is increase of divine knowledge. If any man will know the will of Christ, let him do that will. When a young man is put to learn a trade, he does so by working at it, and we learn the truth our Lord teaches by obeying His commands. To reach the shores of heavenly wisdom, every man must work his passage. Holiness is the royal road to scriptural knowledge. We know as much as we do. "If any man will do his will, he shall know of the doctrine" (John 7:17 KJV). It may be you sit down and consider the doctrine, but you cannot understand it. You turn it over and consult a learned divine, but still you cannot understand it. Be obedient, pray for a willing heart to do the will of God, and you have already received enlarged capacity, and with it, a new light for your eyes. You will learn more by holy practice than by wearisome study. The Lord help us to follow on to know the Lord, for then shall we know! Practice makes perfect. Obedience is the best of schools, and love is the most apt of teachers. To know the love of Christ, which passes knowledge, is the gift of grace to the faithful. Is not this a great reward?

Moreover, in keeping the commandments, we increase in conformity to Christ, and consequently in communion with

God. He that does what Christ did is like Christ; for our likeness is moral and spiritual. In measure, we receive His image as we work His deeds, and then, as Christ lived in constant fellowship with God, because He did always the things that pleased God, so do we walk in the light, as God is in the light, when we yield obedience to the divine will. If you walk in sin, you cannot walk with God. If you will be obedient, then shall all clouds be chased away, and your light shall shine brighter and brighter unto the perfect day. Sinning will make you leave off communion with God, or else communion with God will make you leave off sinning: one of the two things must occur. If you be kept from sin and made to be obedient, you shall bear the image of the heavenly, and with the heavenly, you shall have daily interaction.

This will be followed by the fourth great reward, namely power in prayer. Jesus says, "If you abide in Me, and My words abide in you, you will ask what you desire, and it shall be done for you" (John 15:7). If you will read in the Gospel of John, you will frequently see how success in prayer is, in the case of the believer, made to depend upon his complete obedience. If you will not hearken to God's Word, neither will He hearken to your word. Some people complain that they have no power with God. But has God any power with them? Look to the faultiness of your lives and cease to wonder at the failure of your prayers. An inconsistent life downstairs means unprofitable prayer upstairs—if indeed there be any prayer at all. You cannot have God's ear in the closet if He never has your ear in the shop. If you live as worldlings live, the Lord will treat you as He did

Cain, to whose offering He had no respect. Wonder not at your leanness in private devotion if there is license in your public life. O Lord God the Holy Ghost, sanctify us in our daily lives so we shall obtain access to God through Jesus Christ, and our pleading shall be accepted in Him.

One great reward is habitude in holiness. The man who has, by divine grace, long kept the way of the Lord, finds it easier to do so because he has acquired the habit of obedience. All things are difficult at the beginning, but all things grow easy as we proceed. I do not say that holiness is ever easy to us. It must always be a labor, and we must always be helped by the Holy Spirit, but at the same time, it is far easier for a man to obey who has obeyed than for one to obey who has lived in constant rebellion.

If you have faith, you will have more faith almost as a necessary consequence. If you pray much, you will pray more; it is all but inevitable that you shouldst do so. There are believers whom the Lord has put on the rails of life; they do not run on the road, like common vehicles, but they are placed on tram lines of habit, and so they keep the ways of the Lord. Sometimes a stone gets into the rails, and there is an unhappy jolt, but still they do no iniquity but keep on in one straight line even to their journey's end. This is a great reward of grace.

If you are obedient, you shall be rewarded by being made more obedient. As the diligent workman becomes expert in his art, so shall you grow skillful in holiness. Use is second nature. What a joy it is when holiness becomes our second nature, when prayer becomes habitual as breathing, and praise is as continual as our heartbeats! May hatred to sin be spontaneous and may desire for the best things be the habit of our soul! I scarcely know of a greater reward than this habitude of holiness that the Lord in His grace bestows on us.

This will generally be followed by another great reward, namely, usefulness to others. He who keeps the commandments of the Lord will become an example that others may copy, and he will wield an influence that shall constrain them to copy him. Do not you think that many Christians are spiritually childless because they are disobedient? How can God give me to bring others to Himself if I myself backslide from Him? The power to bless others must first be a power within ourselves. It is useless to pump yourself up into a pretended earnestness at a meeting and then to think that this sort of thing will work a real work of grace in others; the seed of pretense will yield a harvest of pretenders and nothing more.

Nothing can come out of a man unless it is first in him; and if it is in him, it will be seen in his life as well as in his teaching. If I do not live as I preach, my preaching is not living preaching. I could indicate men of great talent who see no conversions, and one does not wonder, for in their own lives there is no holiness, no spirituality, no communion with God. I could mention Christian people, with considerable gifts, who have no corresponding measure of grace, and hence their labor comes to nothing. Oh, for more holiness! Where that is manifest there will be more usefulness.

Last, we shall have the great reward of bringing glory to the grace of God. If we are made holy, men, seeing our good works, will glorify our Father who is in heaven; and is not this the very end of our existence? Is not this the flower and fruit of life? I pray you, therefore, walk humbly and carefully with God that He may be honored in you.

There are two things I want to say before I sit down. The first is, let us hold fast, tenaciously, doggedly, with a death grip the truth of the inspiration of God's Word. If it is not inspired and infallible, it cannot be of use in warning us. I see little use in being warned when the warning may be like the idle cry of "Wolf!" when there is no wolf. Everything in the railway service depends upon the accuracy of the signals: when these are wrong, life will be sacrificed. On the road to heaven, we need unerring signals, or the catastrophes will be far more terrible. It is difficult enough to set myself right and carefully drive the train of conduct. If, in addition to this, I am to set the Bible right and thus manage the signals along the permanent way, I am on an evil plight indeed. If the red light or the green light may deceive me, I am as well without signals as to trust to such faulty guides. We must have something fixed and certain, or where is the foundation? Where is the fulcrum for our lever if nothing is certain? If I may not implicitly trust my Bible, you may burn it, for it is of no more use to me. If it is not inspired, it ceases to be a power either to warn or to command obedience.

While you hold fast its inspiration, pray God to prove its inspiration to you. Its gentle but effectual warning will prove its inspiration. This precious Book has pulled me up many times and put me to a pause, when else I had gone on to sin. At another time I should have sat still had it not made me leap to my feet to flee from evil or seek good. To me it is a monitor whose voice I prize. There is a power about this Book that is not in any other. Nothing ever plays on the cords of a man's soul like the finger of God's Spirit. This Book can touch the deep springs of my being and make the life floods to flow forth. The Word of God is the great power of God, and it is well that you should know it to be so by its power over you. May the Lord work in us to will and to do of His own good pleasure, then shall the Book be more and more precious in our eyes, and this sense of its preciousness will be one of the rewards that come to us in keeping the statutes of the Lord. So be it unto you through Christ Jesus! Amen.

TITLE:

How to Read the Bible

TEXT:

Matthew 12:3–7

SUMMARY:

If we do not understand the Bible, we have not truly read it. Spurgeon's first point is that *in order to achieve the true reading of the Scriptures, there must be an understanding of them*. The benefit of reading the Word is understanding it. For this end we should always pray. Next, Spurgeon says *in reading, we ought to seek out the spiritual teaching of the Word*. Spurgeon makes the argument that *such a reading is profitable*. Reading the Word often begets life.

NOTABLE QUOTES

"Certainly, the benefit of reading must come to the soul by the way of the understanding."

"The Word of God is always most precious to the man who most lives upon it."

"You have not read till you understand the spirit of the matter."

A sermon preached by Charles H. Spurgeon in 1879. *Metropolitan Tabernacle Pulpit*, vol. 25.

7

How to Read
the Bible

*"Have you not read? . . . have you not read? . . .
if you had known what this means . . ."*

MATTHEW 12:3–7

THE SCRIBES AND PHARISEES were great readers of the law. They studied the sacred books continually, poring over each word and letter. They made notes of very little importance, but still very curious notes—as to which was the middle verse of the entire Old Testament, which verse was halfway to the middle, and how many times such a word occurred, and even how many times a letter occurred, and the size of the letter, and its peculiar position. They have left us a mass of wonderful notes upon the mere words of Holy Scripture. They might have done the same thing upon another book, and the information would have been about as important as the facts they have so industriously collected concerning the letter of the

Old Testament. They were, however, intense readers of the law.

They picked a quarrel with the Savior upon a matter touching this law, for they carried it at their fingers' ends and were ready to use it as a bird of prey does its talons to tear and rend. Our Lord's disciples had plucked some ears of corn and rubbed them between their hands. According to Pharisaic interpretation, to rub an ear of corn is a kind of threshing, and, as it is wrong to thresh on the Sabbath day, therefore it must be very wrong to rub out an ear or two of wheat when you are hungry on the Sabbath morning. That was their argument, and they came to the Savior with it and with their version of the Sabbath law.

The Savior generally carried the war into the enemy's camp, and He did so on this occasion. He met them on their own ground, and He said to them, "Have you not read?"—a cutting question to the scribes and Pharisees, though there is nothing apparently sharp about it. It was a fair and proper question to put to them; but only think of putting it to *them*. "Have you not read?"

"Read!" they could have said, "Why, we have read the book through very many times. We are always reading it. No passage escapes our critical eyes."

Yet our Lord proceeds to put the question a second time: "Have you not read?" as if they had not read after all, though they were the greatest readers of the law then living. He insinuates that they have not read at all, and then He gives them, incidentally, the reason why He had asked them whether they had read. He says, "If you had known what this means," as much as to say, "You have not read, because you have not understood."

Your eyes have gone over the words, and you have counted the letters, and you have marked the position of each verse and word, and you have said learned things about all the books, and yet you are not even readers of the sacred volume, for you have not acquired the true art of reading. You do not understand, and therefore you do not truly read it. You are mere skimmers and glancers at the Word; you have not read it, for you do not understand it.

THERE MUST BE AN UNDERSTANDING OF THE SCRIPTURES

I scarcely need to preface these remarks by saying that we must read the Scriptures. You know how necessary it is that we should be fed upon the truth of Holy Scripture. Need I suggest the question as to whether you do read your Bibles or not? I am afraid that this is a magazine-reading age, a newspaper-reading age, a periodical-reading age, but not so much a Bible-reading age as it ought to be.

In the old Puritan times, men used to have a scant supply of other literature, but they found a library enough in the one book: the Bible. And how they did read the Bible! How little of Scripture there is in modern sermons compared with the sermons of those masters of theology, the Puritan divines! Almost every sentence of theirs seems to cast side lights upon a text of Scripture, not only the one they are preaching about but many others as well are set in a new light as the discourse proceeds. They introduce blended lights from other passages that are parallel or semi-parallel thereunto, and thus, they educate their readers to compare spiritual things with spiritual. I would to God that we ministers kept more closely to the grand old Book. We should be instructive preachers if we did so, even if we were ignorant of "modern thought" and were not "abreast of the times." I warrant you we should be leagues ahead of our times if we kept closely to the Word of God.

As for you, my brothers and sisters, who have not to preach, the best food for you is the Word of God itself. Sermons and books are well enough, but streams that run for a long distance above ground gradually gather for themselves somewhat of the soil through which they flow, and they lose the cool freshness with which they started from the spring head. Truth is sweetest where it breaks from the smitten Rock, for at its first gush, it has lost none of its heavenliness and vitality. It is always best to drink at the well and not from the tank. You shall find that reading the Word of God for yourselves, reading it rather than notes upon it, is the surest way of growing in grace. Drink of the unadulterated milk of the Word of God, and not of the skim milk, or the milk and water of man's word.

But, now, beloved, our point is that much apparent Bible reading is not Bible reading at all. The verses pass under the eye, and the sentences glide over the mind, but there is no true reading. An old preacher used to say that the Word has mighty free course among many nowadays, for it goes in at one of their ears and out at the other. So it seems to be with some readers—they can read a very great deal because they do not read anything. The eye glances, but the mind never rests. The soul does not light upon the truth and stay there. It flits over the landscape as a bird might do, but it builds no nest there and finds no rest for the sole of its foot. Such reading is not reading.

Understanding the metering is the essence of true reading. Reading has a kernel to it, and the mere shed is little worth. In prayer there is such a thing as praying in prayer—a praying that is in the bowels of the prayer. So in praise, there is a praising in song, an inward fire of intense devotion, which is the life of the hallelujah. It is so in fasting—there is a fasting that is not fasting, and there is an inward fasting, a fasting of the soul, which is the soul of fasting. It is even so with the reading of the Scriptures. There is an interior reading, a kernel reading—a true and living reading of the Word. This is the soul of reading. If it be not there, the reading is a mechanical exercise and profits nothing.

Now, beloved, unless we understand what we read, we have not read it; the heart of the reading is absent. We commonly condemn the Romanists for keeping the daily service in the Latin tongue, yet it might as well be in the Latin language as in any other tongue if it be not understood by the people. Some comfort themselves with the idea that they have done a good action when they have read a chapter, into the meaning of which they have not entered at all. But does not nature herself reject this as a mere superstition? If you had turned the book upside down and spent the same times in looking at the characters in that direction, you would have gained as much good from it as you will in reading it in the regular way without understanding it. If you had a New Testament in Greek, it would be very Greek to some of you, but it would do you as much good to look at that as it does to look at the English New Testament unless you read with an understanding heart.

It is not the letter that saves the soul; the letter kills in many senses, and never can it give life. If you harp on the letter alone, you may be tempted to use it as a weapon against the truth, as the Pharisees did of old, and your knowledge of the letter may breed pride in you to your destruction. It is the spirit, the real inner meaning that is sucked into the soul, by which we are blessed and sanctified. We become saturated with the Word of God, like Gideon's fleece, which was wet with the dew of heaven. This can only come to pass by our receiving it into our minds and hearts, accepting it as God's truth, and so far understanding it as to delight in it. We must understand it, then, or else we have not read it aright.

Certainly, the benefit of reading must come to the soul by the way of the understanding. When the high priest went into the holy place, he always lit the golden candlestick before he kindled the incense upon the brazen altar, as if to show that the mind must have illumination before the affections can properly rise towards their divine object. There must be knowledge of God before there can be love to God. There must be a knowledge of divine things, as they are revealed, before there can be an enjoyment of them. We must try to make out, as far as our finite mind can grasp it, what God means by this and what He means by that; otherwise, we may kiss the book and have no love to its contents, we may reverence the letter and yet really have no devotion toward the Lord who speaks to us in these words. Beloved, you will never get comfort to your soul out of what you do not understand, nor find guidance for your life out of what you do not comprehend, nor can any practical bearing upon your character come out of what you do not understand.

Now, if we are thus to understand what we read or otherwise we read in vain, this shows us that when we come to the study of Holy Scripture, we should try to have our mind well awake to it. We are not always fit, it seems to me, to read the Bible. At times it would be well for us to stop before we open the volume and "take your sandals off your feet, for the place where you stand is holy ground" (Ex. 3:5). You have just come in from careful thought and anxiety about your worldly business, and you cannot immediately take that Book and enter into its heavenly mysteries. As you ask a blessing over your meat before you fall to, so it would be a good rule for you to ask a blessing on the Word before you partake of its heavenly food. Pray the Lord to strengthen your eyes before you dare to look into the eternal light of Scripture. As the priests washed their feet at the laver before they went to their holy work, so it were well to wash the soul's eyes with which you look upon God's Word, to wash even the fingers—the mental fingers with which you will turn from page to page—that with a holy book you may deal after a holy fashion.

Say to your soul: "Come, soul, wake up: you are not now about to read the newspaper; you are not now perusing the pages of a human poet to be dazzled by his flashing poetry; you are coming very near to God, who sits in the Word like a crowned monarch in his halls. Wake up, my glory; wake up, all that is within me. Though just now I may not be praising and glorifying God, I am about to consider that which should lead me so to do, and therefore it is an act of devotion. So be on the stir, my soul. Be on the stir, and bow not sleepily before the awful throne of the Eternal."

Scripture reading is our spiritual mealtime. Sound the gong and call in every faculty to the Lord's own table to feast upon the precious meat that is now to be partaken of, or, rather, ring the church bell as for worship, for the studying of the Holy Scripture ought to be as solemn a deed as when we lift the psalm upon the Sabbath day in the courts of the Lord's house.

If these things be so, you will see at once, dear friends, that if you are to understand what you read, you will need to meditate upon it. Some passages of Scripture lie clear before us—blessed shallows in which the lambs may wade. But there are deeps in which our mind might rather drown herself than swim with pleasure if she came there without caution. There are texts of Scripture that are made and constructed on purpose to make us think. By this means, among others, our heavenly Father would educate us for heaven—by making us think our way into divine mysteries. Hence He puts the word in a somewhat involved form to compel us to meditate upon it before we reach the sweetness of it. He might, you know, have explained it to us so that we might catch the thought in a minute, but He does not please to do so in every case.

Many of the veils that are cast over Scripture are not meant to hide the meaning from the diligent but to compel the mind to be active, for oftentimes, the diligence of the heart in seeking to know the divine mind does the heart more good than the knowledge itself. Meditation and careful thought exercise us and strengthen us for the reception of the yet more lofty truths.

I have heard that the mothers in the Balearic Isles, in the old times, who wanted to bring their boys up to be good slingers, would put their dinners up above them where they could not get at them until they threw a stone and fetched them down. Our Lord wishes us to be good slingers, and He puts up some precious truth in a lofty place where we cannot get it down except by slinging at it. At last, we hit the mark and find food for our souls. Then have we the double benefit of learning the art of meditation and partaking of the sweet truth that it has brought within our reach.

We must meditate, brothers. These grapes will yield no wine till we tread upon them. These olives must be put under the wheel and pressed again and again that the oil may flow therefrom. In a dish of nuts, you may know which nut has been eaten because there is a little hole that the insect has punctured through the shell—just a little hole, and then inside there is the living thing eating up the kernel. Well, it is a grand thing to bore through the shell of the letter and then to live inside feeding upon the kernel. I would wish to be such a little worm as that, living within and upon the Word of God, having bored my way through the shell and having reached the innermost mystery of the blessed gospel.

The Word of God is always most precious to the man who most lives upon it. As I sat last year under a wide-spreading beech, I was pleased to mark with prying curiosity the singular habits of that most wonderful of trees, which seems to have an intelligence about it which other trees have not. I wondered and admired the beech, but I thought to myself, I do not think half as much of this beech tree as yonder squirrel does. I see him leap from bough to bough, and I feel sure that he dearly values the old beech tree because he has his home somewhere inside it in a hollow place; these branches are his shelter, and those beech-nuts are his food. He lives upon the tree. It is his world, his playground, his granary, his home; indeed, it is everything to him, and it is not so to me, for I find my rest and food elsewhere.

With God's Word, it is well for us to be like squirrels, living in it and living on it. Let us exercise our minds by leaping from bough to bough of it, find our rest and food in it, and make it our all in all. We shall be the people that get the profit out of it if we make it to be our food, our medicine, our treasury, our armory, our rest, our delight. May the Holy Ghost lead us to do this and make the Word thus precious to our souls.

Beloved, I would next remind you that for this end, we shall be compelled to pray. It is a grand thing to be driven to think; it is a grander thing to be driven to pray through having been made to think. Am I not addressing some of you who do not read the Word of God, and am I not speaking to many more who do read it but not with the strong resolve that they will understand it? I know it must be so. Do you wish to begin to be true readers? Will you henceforth labor to understand? Then you must get to your knees. You must cry to God for direction.

Who understands a book best? The author of it. If I want to ascertain the real meaning of a rather twisted sentence, and the author lives near me, and I can call upon him, I shall ring at his door and say, "Would you kindly tell me what you mean by that sentence? I have no doubt whatever that it is very clear but I am such a simpleton that I cannot make it out. I have not the knowledge and grasp of the subject you possess, and therefore your allusions and descriptions are beyond my range of knowledge. It is quite within your range, and commonplace to you, but it is very difficult to me. Would you kindly explain your meaning to me?"

A good man would be glad to be thus treated and would think it no trouble to unravel his meaning to a candid enquirer. Thus I should be sure to get the correct meaning, for I should be going to the fountainhead when I consulted the author himself. So, beloved, the Holy Spirit is with us, and when we take His book and begin to read and want to know what it means, we must ask the Holy Spirit to reveal the meaning. He will not work a miracle, but He will elevate our minds, and He will suggest to us thoughts that will lead us on by their natural relation, the one to the other, till at last we come to the pith and marrow of His divine instruction. Seek then earnestly the guidance of the Holy Spirit, for if the very soul of reading be the understanding of what we read, then we must in prayer call upon the Holy Ghost to unlock the secret mysteries of the inspired Word.

If we thus ask the guidance and teaching of the Holy Spirit, it will follow, dear friends, that we shall be ready to use all means toward the understanding of the Scriptures. When Philip asked the Ethiopian eunuch whether he understood the prophecy of Isaiah, he replied, "How can I, unless someone guides me?" (Acts 8:31). Then Philip went up and opened to him the Word of the Lord.

Some, under the pretense of being taught of the Spirit of God, refuse to be instructed by books or by living men. This is no honoring of the Spirit of God; it is a disrespect to Him, for if He gives to some of His servants more light than to others—and it is clear He does—then they are bound to give that light to others and to use it for the good of the church. But if the other part of the church refuses to receive that light, to what end did the Spirit of God give it? This would imply that there is a mistake somewhere in the economy of gifts and graces, which is managed by the Holy Spirit. It cannot be so. The Lord Jesus Christ pleases to give more knowledge of His Word and more insight into it to some of His servants than to others, and it is ours joyfully to accept the knowledge which He gives in such ways as He chooses to give it.

It would be most wicked of us to say, "We will not have the heavenly treasure that exists in earthen vessels. If God will give us the heavenly treasure out of His own hand, but not through the earthen vessel, we will have it; but we think we are too wise, too heavenly minded, too spiritual altogether to care for jewels when they are placed in earthen pots. We will not hear anybody, and we will not read anything except the book itself, neither will we accept any light, except that which comes in through a crack in our own roof. We will not see by another man's candle; we would sooner remain in the dark."

Brethren, do not let us fall into such folly. Let the light come from God, and though a child shall bring it, we will joyfully accept it. If any one of His servants, whether Paul or Apollos or Cephas, shall have received light from Him, behold, "all are yours. And you are Christ's, and Christ is God's" (1 Cor. 3:22–23). Therefore, accept of the light God has kindled and ask for grace that you may turn that light upon the Word so that when you read it, you may understand it.

I do not wish to say much more about this, but I should like to push it home upon some of you. You have Bibles at home, I know. You would not like to be without Bibles; you would think you were heathens if you had no Bibles. You have them very neatly bound, and they are very fine-looking volumes; not much thumbed, not much worn, and not likely to be so, for they only come out on Sundays for an airing, and they lie in lavender with the clean pocket handkerchiefs all the rest of the week.

You do not read the Word, you do not search it, and how can you expect to get the divine blessing? If the heavenly gold is not worth digging for, you are not likely to discover it. Often and often have I told you that the searching of the Scriptures is not the way of salvation. The Lord has said, "Believe on the Lord Jesus Christ, and you will be saved" (Acts 16:31). But still, the reading of the Word often leads, like the hearing of it, to faith, and faith brings salvation; for faith comes by hearing, and reading is a sort of hearing. While you are seeking to know what the gospel is, it may please God to bless your souls. But what poor reading some of you give to your Bibles.

I do not want to say anything that is too severe because it is not strictly true—let your own consciences speak, but still, I make bold to enquire: Do not many of you read the Bible in a hurried way—just a little bit, and off you go? Do you not soon forget what you have read and lose what little effect it seemed to have? How few of you are resolved to get at its soul, its juice, its life, its essence, and to drink in its meaning! Well, if you do not do that, I tell you again, your reading is miserable, dead, unprofitable reading; it is not reading at all, the name would be misapplied. May the blessed Spirit give you repentance touching this thing.

SEEK OUT THE SPIRITUAL TEACHING
OF THE WORD

I think that is in my text because our Lord says, "Have you not read?" Then again, "Have you not read?" and then He says, "If you had known what this means"—and the meaning is something very spiritual. The text He quoted was, "I desire mercy and not sacrifice"—a text out of the prophet Hosea. Now, the scribes and Pharisees were all for the letter—the sacrifice, the killing of the bullock, and so on. They overlooked the spiritual meaning of the passage—"I desire mercy and not sacrifice"— namely, that God prefers that we should care for our fellow creatures rather than that we should observe any ceremony of His law, so as to cause hunger or thirst and thereby death to any of the creatures His hands have made. They ought to have passed beyond the outward into the spiritual, and all our readings ought to do the same.

This should be the case when we read the historical passages. "Have you not read what David did when he was hungry, he and those who were with him: how he entered the house of God and ate the showbread which was not lawful for him to eat, nor for those who were with him, but only for the priests?" (Matt. 12:3–4). This was a piece of history, and they ought so to have read it as to have found spiritual instruction in it. I have heard very stupid people say, "Well, I do not care to read the historical parts of Scripture." Beloved friends, you do not know what you are talking about when you say so.

I say to you now by experience that I have sometimes found even a greater depth of spirituality in the histories than I have in the Psalms. You will say, "How is that?" I assert that when you reach the inner and spiritual meaning of a history you are often surprised at the wondrous clearness—the realistic force—with which the teaching comes home to your soul. Some of the most marvelous mysteries of revelation are better understood by being set before our eyes in the histories than they are by the verbal declaration of them.

When we have the statement to explain the illustration, the illustration expands and vivifies the statement. For instance, when our Lord Himself would explain to us what faith was, He sent us to the history of the brazen serpent. Who that has ever read the story of the brazen serpent has not felt that he has had a better idea of faith through the picture of the dying, snake-bitten persons looking to the serpent of brass and living, than from any description that even Paul has given us, wondrously as he defines and describes? Never, I pray you, depreciate the historical portions of God's Word, but when you cannot get good out of them, say, "That is my foolish head and my slow heart. O Lord, be pleased to clear my brain and cleanse my soul." When He answers that prayer, you will feel that every portion of God's Word is given by inspiration and is and must be profitable to you.

Just the same thing is true with regard to all the ceremonial precepts, because the Savior goes on to say, "Have you not read in the law that on the Sabbath the priests in the temple profane the Sabbath, and are blameless?" (Matt. 12:5). There is not a single precept in the old law but has an inner sense and meaning; therefore, do not turn away from Leviticus, or say, "I cannot read these chapters in the books of Exodus and Numbers. They are all about the tribes and their standards, the stations in the wilderness and the halts of the march, the tabernacle and furniture, or about golden knobs and bowls, and boards, and sockets, and precious stones, and blue and scarlet and fine linen."

No, but look for the inner meaning. Make thorough search. For as in a king's treasure that which is the most closely locked up and the hardest to come at is the choicest jewel of the treasure, so is it with the Holy Scriptures. Did you ever go to the British Museum Library? There are many books of reference there that the reader is allowed to take down when he pleases. There are other books for which he must write a ticket, and he cannot get them without the ticket. But they have certain choice books that you will not see without a special order, and then there is an unlocking of doors, and an opening of cases, and there is a watcher with you while you make your inspection. You are scarcely allowed to put your eye on the manuscript, for fear you should blot a letter out by glancing at it. It is such a precious treasure; there is not another copy of it in all the world, and so you cannot get at it easily.

Just so, there are choice and precious doctrines of God's Word that are locked up in such cases as Leviticus or Solomon's Song, and you cannot get at them without a deal of unlocking of doors, and the Holy Spirit Himself must be with you or else you will never come at the priceless treasure. The higher truths are as choicely hidden away as the precious regalia of princes; therefore search as well as read. Do not be satisfied with a ceremonial precept till you reach its spiritual meaning, for that is true reading. You have not read till you understand the spirit of the matter.

It is just the same with the doctrinal statements of God's Word. I have sorrowfully observed some persons who are very orthodox and who can repeat their creed very glibly, and yet the principal use that they make of their orthodoxy is to sit and watch the preacher with the view of framing a charge against him. He has uttered a single sentence that is judged to be half a hair's breadth below the standard: "That man is not sound. He said some good things, but he is rotten at the core, I am certain. He used an expression that was not eighteen ounces to the pound." Sixteen ounces to the pound are not enough for these dear brethren of whom I speak; they must have something more and over and above the shekel of the sanctuary. Their knowledge is used as a microscope to magnify trifling differences.

I hesitate not to say that I have come across persons who "Could a hair divide, Betwixt the west and north-west side," in matters of divinity but who know nothing about the things of God in their real meaning. They have never drunk them into their souls but only sucked them up into their mouths to spit them out on others. The doctrine of election is one thing, but to know that God has predestined you, and to have the fruit of it in the good works to which you are ordained, is quite another thing. To talk about the love of Christ, to talk about the heaven that is provided for His people, and such things—all this is very well. But this may be done without any personal acquaintance with them. Therefore, beloved, never be satisfied with a sound creed, but desire to have it graven on the tablets of your heart. The doctrines of grace are good, but the grace of the doctrines is better still. See that you have it, and be not content with the idea that you are instructed until you so understand the doctrine that you have felt its spiritual power.

This makes us feel that, in order to come to this, we shall need to feel Jesus present with us whenever we read the Word. Mark that fifth verse, which I would now bring before you as part of my text that I have hitherto left out. "Have you not read in the law that on the Sabbath the priests in the temple profane the Sabbath, and are blameless? Yet I say to you that in this place there is One greater than the temple" (Matt. 12:5–6). Ay, they thought much about the letter of the Word, but they did not know that He was there who is the Sabbath's Master— man's Lord and the Sabbath's Lord, and Lord of everything.

Oh, when you have got hold of a creed, or of an ordinance, or anything that is outward in the letter, pray the Lord to make you feel that there is something greater than the printed book and something better than the mere shell of the creed. There is one person greater than them all, and to Him we should cry that He may be ever with us. O living Christ, make this a living Word to me. Your Word is life, but not without the Holy Spirit. I may know this Book of yours from beginning to end, and repeat it all from Genesis to Revelation, and yet it may be a dead book, and I may be a dead soul. But, Lord, be present here. Then will I look up from the Book to the Lord; from the precept to Him who fulfilled it; from the law to Him who honored it; from the threatening to Him who has borne it for me, and from the promise to Him in whom it is "Yes and amen."

Ah, then we shall read the book so differently. He is here with me in this chamber of mine. I must not trifle. He leans over me, He puts his finger along the lines, I can see His pierced hand. I will read it as in His presence. I will read it, knowing that He is the substance of it, that He is the proof of this Book as well as the writer of it; the sum of this Scripture as well as the author of it. That is the way for true students to become wise! You will get at the soul of Scripture when you can keep Jesus with you while you are reading.

Did you never hear a sermon as to which you felt that if Jesus had come into that pulpit while the man was making his oration, He would have said, "Go down, go down; what business have you here? I sent you to preach about me, and you preach about a dozen other things. Go home and learn of me, and then come and talk." That sermon that does not lead to Christ, or of which Jesus Christ is not the top and the bottom, is a sort of sermon that will make the devils in hell laugh but might make the angel of God to weep, if they were capable of such emotion.

You remember the story I told you of the Welshman who heard a young man preach a very fine sermon—a grand sermon, a highfalutin, spread-eagle sermon. And when he had done, he asked the Welshman what he thought of it. The man replied that he did not think anything of it.

"And why not?"

"Because there was no Jesus Christ in it."

"Well," said he, "but my text did not seem to run that way."

"Never mind," said the Welshman, "your sermon ought to run that way."

"I do not see that, however," said the young man.

"No," said the Welshman, "you do not see how to preach yet. This is the way to preach. From every little village in England—it does not matter where it is—there is sure to be a road to London. Though there may not be a road to certain other places, there is certain to be a road to London. Now, from every text in the Bible there is a road to Jesus Christ, and the way to preach is just to say, 'How can I get from this text to Jesus Christ?' and then go preaching all the way along it."

"Well, but," said the young man, "suppose I find a text that has not got a road to Jesus Christ."

"I have preached for forty years," said the old man, "and I have never found such a Scripture, but if I ever do find one, I will go over hedge and ditch but what I will get to Him, for I will never finish without bringing in my Master."

Perhaps you will think that I have gone a little over hedge and ditch tonight, but I am persuaded that I have not, for the sixth verse comes in here and brings our Lord in most sweetly, setting Him in the very forefront of you Bible readers so that you must not think of reading without feeling that He is there who is Lord and Master of everything that you are reading and who shall make these things precious to you if you realize Him in them.

If you do not find Jesus in the Scriptures, they will be of small service to you, for what did our Lord Himself say? "You search the Scriptures, for in them you think you have eternal life. . . . But you are not willing to come to Me that you may have life" (John 5:39–40), and therefore your searching comes to nothing. You find no life and remain dead in your sins. May it not be so with us.

SUCH A READING OF SCRIPTURE IS PROFITABLE

Such a reading of Scripture that implies the understanding of and entrance into its spiritual meaning, along with the discovery of the divine Person who is the spiritual meaning, is profitable, for here our Lord says, "If you had known what this means, 'I desire mercy and not sacrifice,' you would not have condemned the guiltless." It will save us from making a great many mistakes if we get to understand the Word of God, and among other good things we shall not condemn the guiltless.

I have no time to enlarge upon these benefits, but I will just say, putting all together, that the diligent reading of the Word of God with the strong resolve to get at its meaning often begets spiritual life. We are begotten by the Word of God: it is the instrumental means of regeneration. Therefore, love your

Bibles. Keep close to your Bibles. You seeking sinners, you who are seeking the Lord, your first business is to believe in the Lord Jesus Christ, but while you are yet in darkness and in gloom, love your Bibles and search them! Take them to bed with you, and when you wake up in the morning, if it is too early to go downstairs and disturb the house, get half an hour of reading upstairs. Say, "Lord, guide me to that text which shall bless me. Help me to understand how I, a poor sinner, can be reconciled to You."

I recollect how, when I was seeking the Lord, I went to my Bible and to Baxter's "Call to the Unconverted," and to Allen's "Alarm," and Doddridge's "Rise and Progress," for I said in myself, "I am afraid that I shall be lost, but I will know the reason why. I am afraid I never shall find Christ, but it shall not be for want of looking for Him." That fear used to haunt me, but I said, "I will find Him if He is to be found. I will read. I will think."

There was never a soul that did sincerely seek for Jesus in the Word but by-and-by he stumbled on the precious truth that Christ was near at hand and did not want any looking for. That He was really there, only they, poor blind creatures, were in such a maze that they could not just then see Him. Oh, cling to Scripture. Scripture is not Christ, but it is the silken clue that will lead you to Him. Follow its leadings faithfully.

When you have received regeneration and a new life, keep on reading, because it will comfort you. You will see more of what the Lord has done for you. You will learn that you are redeemed, adopted, saved, sanctified. Half the errors in the world spring from people not reading their Bibles. Would anybody think that the Lord would leave any one of His dear children to perish if he read such a text as this: "I give them eternal life, and they shall never perish; neither shall anyone snatch them out of My hand" (John 10:28)? When I read that, I am sure of the final perseverance of the saints. Read the Word, and it will be much for your comfort. It will be for your nourishment, too. It is your food as well as your life. Search it, and you will grow strong in the Lord and in the power of His might.

It will be for your guidance also. I am sure those go rightest who keep closest to the Book. Oftentimes, when you do not know what to do, you will see a text leaping up out of the Book and saying, "Follow me." I have seen a promise sometimes blaze out before my eyes just as when an illuminated device flames forth upon a public building. One touch of flame, and a sentence or a design flashes out. I have seen a text of Scripture flame forth in that way to my soul; I have known that it was God's word to me, and I have gone on my way rejoicing.

And, oh, you will get a thousand helps out of that wondrous Book if you do but read it; for, understanding the words more, you will prize it more. And as you get older, the Book will grow with your growth and turn out to be a greybeard's manual of devotion just as it was aforetime a child's sweet story book.

Yes, it will always be a new Book—just as new a Bible as it was printed yesterday and nobody had ever seen a word of it till now—and yet it will be a deal more precious for all the memories that cluster round it. As we turn over its pages, how sweetly do we recollect passages in our history that will never be forgotten to all eternity but will stand forever intertwined with gracious promises. Beloved, the Lord teach us to read His book of life that He has opened before us here below, so that we may read our titles clear in that other book of love that we have not seen as yet but that will be opened at the last great day. The Lord be with you and bless you.

Acknowledgments

As with any writing project, this book would not have come to completion without the sacrifice and support of many. I remain profoundly indebted to each one of them.

At the personal level, my life and ministry are enabled and enriched by the prayers and encouragement of my family. God has given me a wife, Karen, and children, Anne-Marie, Caroline, William, Alden, and Elizabeth, who bless me beyond measure. I love each one of you unconditionally and beyond measure.

At the institutional level, my colleagues and office staff likewise are an invaluable source of support and encouragement. Most especially, I'm thankful for Tyler Sykora, Dawn Philbrick, Lauren Hanssen, Wesley Rule, and Justin Love. I'm also thankful for Russ Meek, who provided keen editorial assistance. Each one of these men and women is an absolute delight to serve with, and they each go about their daily tasks with graciousness and competence. Thank you.

I'm thankful to the team at Moody Publishers, most especially Drew Dyck and Kevin Mungons. Thank you for believing in this project and for working with me to bring it to completion.

Last, and most of all, I'm indebted to my Lord and Savior, Jesus Christ. Like every other ministerial undertaking, none of this would be possible without His grace, calling, and enabling. May this book, and all that I do, bring Him much glory.

When Spurgeon speaks, you'd be wise to listen.

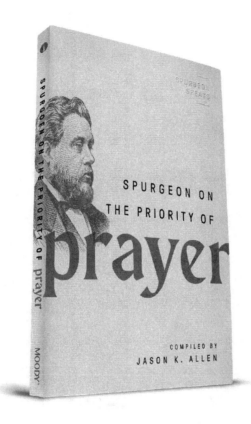

Collected insights from A.W. Tozer on common topics for the Christian life

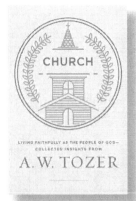
978-0-8024-1828-9

978-1-60066-801-2

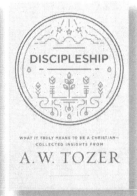
978-1-60066-804-3

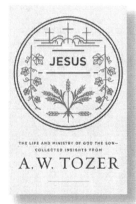
978-0-8024-1520-2

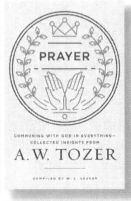
978-0-8024-1381-9

978-0-8024-1603-2

also available as eBooks

MOODY
Publishers®

From the Word to Life®

"Only God can justify the ungodly, but He can do it to perfection. He casts our sins behind His back; He blots them out. He says that though they be sought for, they shall not be found."

—C. H. SPURGEON

MOODY Publishers®

From the Word to Life®

In an age of limited travel and isolated nations, C. H. Spurgeon preached to over 10,000,000 people in person—sometimes up to ten times per week. It is in this classic work that Spurgeon most clearly presents the message of salvation—man's ultimate need and God's unique provision—both simply and sincerely, for honest seekers and zealous witnesses alike.

978-0-8024-5452-2 | also available as an eBook